Updated 2018

Egyptian Divinities

The All Who Are THE ONE

Expanded Second Edition

Moustafa Gadalla

Tehuti Research Foundation
International Head Office: Greensboro, NC, U.S.A.

D1694685

Egyptian Divinities
The All Who Are THE ONE
Expanded 2nd Edition
by Moustafa Gadalla

Published by:
Tehuti Research Foundation
P.O. Box 39491
Greensboro, NC 27438, U.S.A.

Publisher's Cataloging-in-Publication

Gadalla, Moustafa, 1944-
Egyptian divinities: the all who are the One/
Moustafa Gadalla.—2nd ed.
p. cm.
Includes bibliographical references.

LCCN: 2016930020
ISBN-13 (PDF): 978-1-931446-57-0
ISBN-13 (e-book): 978-1-931446- 58-7
ISBN-13 (pbk.): 978-1-931446-59-4

1. Gods, Egyptian. 2. Egypt—Religion. 3. Occultism—Egypt. 4. Egypt—Civilization. 5. Cosmology, Egyptian. I. Title.
BL2450.G6G33 2017   299'.31

Updated 2018

CONTENTS

ABOUT THE AUTHOR

Moustafa Gadalla is an Egyptian-American independent Egyptologist who was born in Cairo, Egypt in 1944. He holds a Bachelor of Science degree in civil engineering from Cairo University.

Gadalla is the author of twenty-two published internationally acclaimed books about the various aspects of the Ancient Egyptian history and civilization and its influences worldwide.

He is the Founder and Chairman of the Tehuti Research Foundation (https://www.egypt-tehuti.org)—an international, U.S.-based, non-profit organization, dedicated to Ancient Egyptian studies. He is also the Founder and Head of the online Egyptian Mystical University (https://www.EgyptianMysticalUniversity.org).

From his early childhood, Gadalla pursued his Ancient Egyptian roots with passion, through continuous study and research. Since 1990, he has dedicated and concentrated all his time to researching and writing.

PREFACE [1ST EDITION]

The most common knowledge about Ancient Egyptian divinities comes to us as the result of the "interpretation" by western academic Egyptologists of the Ancient Egyptian texts. Their "interpretations" are constrained by their Western and Judaeo-Christian paradigms. As a result, they report a confused religious system with a great number of (so-called) "gods".

Academic Egyptologists, while worshipping everything Greek or Roman, totally ignore the eyewitness accounts of Herodotus, Plutarch, Plato, Diodorus, and other historians who reported about the Ancient Egyptian traditions, and who were much closer to the scene than the further-removed Western academic Egyptologists.

This book avoids the paradigms, clears up the confusion, and explains the meaning(s) of over 80 of the most frequently encountered divinities . . .The All Who Are THE ONE.

Moustafa Gadalla
September, 2001

PREFACE [2ND EDITION]

This book is a revised and an enhanced edition of the first edition that was published in 2001.

It should be noted that the digital edition of this book as published in PDF and E-book formats have a substantial number of photographs that compliment the text materials throughout the boo

This Expanded Edition of the book consists of two Parts with a total of 12 Chapters.

Part I: The All Who Are THE ONE consists of seven chapters—1 through 7, as follows:

> *Chapter 1:* **The One is ALL** explains that far from being a primitive, polytheistic form, the Egyptians' ideology is the highest expression of monotheistic mysticism.

> *Chapter 2:* **The Divine Energies of The Creation Cycle** covers the role of the divine energies in the creation cycle which accords with scientific principles; and how such divine energies were recognized in later creeds as 'Angels of God'.

Chapter 3: **Manifestation of Neteru in The Orderly Creation Process** covers such manifestation into three primary phases, in the Egyptian creation process accounts.

Chapter 4: **Understanding Names, Epithets & Titles** covers the real secret names and how Egyptians used epithets and titles when referring to the divine energies.

Chapter 5: **Narration of Their Manifestations** explains how the cosmological knowledge of Ancient Egypt was expressed in a story form, which is a superior means for expressing both physical and metaphysical concepts.

Chapter 6: **Common Misrepresentations of the Divinities in Egypt** covers examples of such misrepresentations and provides the real intended representations.

Chapter 7: **Man and The Divine Forces** covers man's place in the universal order; man as the image of the universe; the two Heavenly Courts; the three primary Heavenly Helpers to earthly dwellers; and man interactions with the divine forces in the Egyptian temples.

Part II : The Roles of Most Recognized Neteru (gods/ goddesses) consists of five chapters—8 through 12, as follows:

Chapter 8: **Mystical Pictorial Depictions** covers pictorial symbolism of the Neteru and how Egyptian depictions reflect metaphysical concepts through the use of human figuration, animal symbolism, accessories, emblems, color, etc.; as well as various action forms.

Chapter 9: **Most Common Animals and Birds Forms Neteru** covers the metaphysical significance of several animal images such as that of the ass, baboon, beetle, Bennu/Benben, bulls, cat, cows [Mehet-Uret (Mehurt, Methyer); Hesat, Hathor], crocodile, dog, egg, falcon, feather, fish, frog, goose, hare, heron, hippopotamus, horse, ibis, lions [lion, lioness & twin-lions (Aker)], Phoenix, rams, serpents, stork, vulture, and winged sun.

Chapter 10: **Most Common Male & Androgynous Human Forms Divinities** covers the metaphysical significance of several male and androgynous human form images such as:
Amon (Amen, Amun), Anubis (Anbu, Ubuat ,Webwawet), Apis (Epaphus, Hapis), Aton (Adon), Atum (Atem, Atom, Atam), Bes, Geb (Seb, Keb), Hapi (Hepr), Herishef (Harsaphis, Arshaphes, Arsaphes), Horus (Heru)—[also Hor-Sa-Auset,/Horsiesis (or Harsiesis), Heru-p-Khart/Hor-Pa-Khred/Harpocrates, Horus Behdety/pollo and Heru-ur/Haroeris/Harueris], Hor.Akhti/Horachti, Khepri (Khepera), Khnum, Khonsu (Khons), Min (Menu, Amsi, Kamutef), Nefertum—[also, The Triad Ptah-Sokaris-Nefertum], Nun/Nu/Ny, Osiris (Ausar, Usire, Asar), Ptah (Phtas, Vulcan), Re (Ra), Re Hor akhti (Rahorakhty), Reshpu (Reshef, Reseph), Sebek, (Sobek, Suchos), Seth (Set,

Sutekh, Typhon), Sokaris (Sokar, Sakar, Seqr), Shu, and Thoth [Tehuti, Hermes, Mercury]

Chapter 11: **Most Common Female Human Forms Divinities** covers the metaphysical significance of several female human form images such as:
Isis (Auset, Ast)—The divine female Principle/Principal, Anat, Bast (Bastet, Oubastis), Heket (Heqet), Hathor (Het-Hor, Het-Heru, Venus, Aphrodite)—[also- Mehet-Uret (Mehurt, Methyer)-Heru-sekha- Hesat – Merit- Tree Netrt (goddess) – Astrate/Asera/Serah/Sarah- Notre Dame], Kadesh (Qadesh), Maat (Mayet), Merit, Mut, Nephthys (Nebt-het), Neith (Net), Nut, Satis (Satet), Sekhmet (Sekh-Mut, Sakhmet, Petesachmis), Selkis (Serket, Selkit, Serqet), Seshat (Safkhet, Sesat, Seshet, Sesheta, Seshata), Taurt (Taweret, Thoeris, Toeris), and Tefnut

Chapter 12: **The Archetypal Synergies** covers the complex and shifting array of
relationships between the divine energies and how such synergies are being manifested in various associations such as dualities, trinities, octads and enneads.

It should be noted that the digital edition of this book as published in PDF and E-book formats have a substantial number of photographs that compliment the text materials throughout the book.

Moustafa Gadalla

STANDARDS AND TERMINOLOGY

1. The Ancient Egyptian word, neter and its feminine form netert have been wrongly, and possibly intentionally, translated to 'god and goddess', by almost all academicians. Neteru (plural of neter/netert) are the divine principles and functions of the One Supreme God.

2. You may find variations in writing the same Ancient Egyptian term, such as Amen/Amon/Amun or Pir/Per. This is because the vowels you see in translated Egyptian texts are only approximations of sounds which are used by Western Egyptologists to help them pronounce the Ancient Egyptian terms/words.

3. We will be using the most commonly recognized words for the English-speaking people that identify a neter/ netert [god, goddess], a pharaoh, or a city; followed by other 'variations' of such a word/term.

It should be noted that the real names of the deities (gods, goddesses) were kept secret so as to guard the cosmic power of the deity. The Neteru were referred to by epithets that describe a particular quality, attribute and/or aspect(s) of their roles. Such applies to all common terms such as Isis, Osiris, Amun, Re, Horus, etc.

4. When using the Latin calendar, we will use the following terms:

> **BCE** – Before Common Era. Also noted in other references as BC.
> **CE** – Common Era. Also noted in other references as AD.

5. The term Baladi will be used throughout this book to denote the present silent majority of Egyptians that adhere to the Ancient Egyptian traditions, with a thin exterior layer of Islam.[See *Ancient Egyptian Culture Revealed* by Moustafa Gadalla for detailed information.]

6. There were/are no Ancient Egyptian writings/texts that were categorized by the Egyptians themselves as "religious", "funerary", "sacred", etc. Western academia gave the Ancient Egyptian texts arbitrary names such as the "Book of This", and the "Book of That", "divisions", "utterances", "spells", etc. Western academia even decided that a certain "Book" had a "Theban version" or "this or that time period version". After believing their own inventive creation, academia then accused the Ancient Egyptians of making mistakes and missing portions of their writings(?!!).

For ease of reference, we will mention the common but arbitrary Western academic categorization of Ancient Egyptian texts, even though the Ancient Egyptians themselves never did.

MAP OF EGYPT

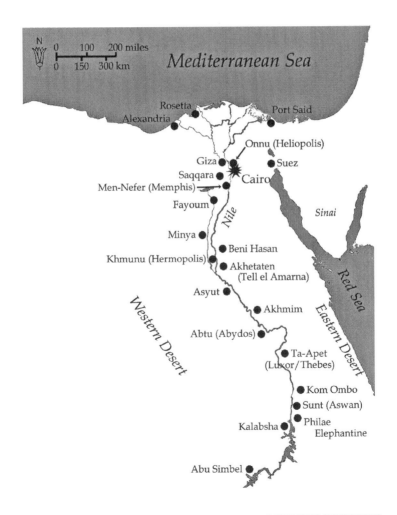

PART I : THE ALL WHO ARE THE ONE

CHAPTER 1 : THE ONE IS ALL

1.1 MONOTHEISM AND POLYTHEISM

So much has been written, asserted, and repeated about how polytheistic the Egyptian religion was; yet it will be a surprise to most that, far from being a primitive, polytheistic form, this is the highest expression of monotheistic mysticism. Moreover, it is as valid now as it was valid then—For the Truth is ETERNAL.

The word/name "God" does not by itself tell us anything. To know "God" is to know the numerous attributes/qualities/powers/actions of "God".

Likewise, the Egyptians regarded the universe as a conscious act of creation by the One Supreme Power. The fundamental doctrine was the unity of the Deity. This One God was never represented. It is the manifestation of the functions and attributes of the One Great God that were represented. Once a reference was made to such any of such functions/attributes, it became a distinguishable agent, reflecting this particular function/attribute and its influence on the world. The various functions and attributes were called the neteru (singular: neter in the masculine form and netert in the feminine form). As such, an Egyptian neter/netert was not a god/goddess but the representation of a function/attribute/powers of the One God.

Far from being a primitive, polytheistic form, this is the highest expression of monotheistic mysticism.

In Ancient Egyptian traditions, Re (Ra) represents the primeval, cosmic, creative force. The Litany describes Re (Ra) as:

> *"The One Joined Together, Who Comes Out of His Own Members."*

The Ancient Egyptian definition of Re is "the perfect representation of the Unity that comprises the multitude of the many diverse entities", i.e. The One Who is the All.

The Litany of Re (Ra) describes the aspects of the creative principle: being recognized as the neteru (gods, goddesses) whose actions and interactions, in turn, created the universe. As such, all the Egyptian neteru who took part in the creation process are aspects of Re (Ra). There are 75 forms or aspects of Re (Ra). Re (Ra) is often incorporated into the names of other neteru (gods) such as in Amen-Re, Re-Atum, Re-Harakhti, etc.

The solar energy of the sun is only one of numerous manifestations of Re (Ra). That Re (Ra) is not just the sun (only a singular form) was also confirmed in the following verse from the Story of *Re and Isis*, in which Re (Ra) states:

> *"I have multitude of names, and multitude of forms."*

1.2 AMEN-RENEF: THE INDEFINABLE

The deeply religious Egyptians, recognizing that no human being can define the indefinable, believed in the presence of an unlimited, unknowable power that is too majestic to communicate with the created universe (but without this power, no creation can exist).

Outside the universe and its cyclical nature is what the Ancient Egyptians referred to as Amen-Renef, which is not a name of any entity, but a sentence that means *'That with Unknown Essence'*. In this realm of the unknowable, no words in any terms of human thought could be spoken, and the deeply religious Egyptians never did. They could only convey *'it'* by negation of all qualities. The Egyptians would say:

> *"Whose name is unknown to all neteru*—[meaning the forces and energies of the universe]
> *Who has no definition,* [i.e. cannot be defined/described in any human term].
> *Who has no image.*
> *Who has no form.*
> *Who has no beginning and no end";* etc., etc.

As such, the Ancient Egyptian expression, Amen-Renef, transcends even the quality of being. Amen-Renef is not the Creator or the First-Cause. All the terms (God, Creator, Master of the Universe, First Cause, The First) are lower principles and are separate from Amen-Renef.

The Egyptians uttered no more of it—and then only under infinite reserve, appealing always to a deep sense behind the words that Amen-Renef is everywhere, in the sense that without its Supra-Existence nothing could be.

Now acknowledging Amen-Renef, whose essence is unknown, we can enter the realms of the creation cycles, of which we are a part.

CHAPTER 2 : NETERU: THE DIVINE ENERGIES OF THE CREATION CYCLE

2.1 IN THE PRE-CREATION BEGINNING—NUN—NOTHINGNESS

Every Egyptian creation text begins with the same basic belief that before the beginning of things, there was a liquidy primeval abyss—everywhere, endless, and without boundaries or directions. Egyptians called this cosmic ocean/watery chaos Nu/Ny/Nun—the un-polarized state of matter. Water is formless, and of itself it does not take on any shape; nor does it resist being shaped (it is infinitely receptive).

Scientists agree with the Ancient Egyptian description of the origin of the universe as being an abyss. Scientists refer to this abyss as *neutron soup*, where there are neither electrons nor protons; only neutrons forming one huge, extremely dense nucleus.

Such chaos, in the pre-creation state, was caused by the compression of matter; i.e. atoms did not exist in their normal states, but were squeezed so closely together that many atomic nuclei were crowded into a space previously occupied by a single normal atom. Under such conditions, the electrons of these atoms were squeezed out of their orbits and moved about freely; i.e. in a chaotic, degenerate state. This represented the un-polarized state of matter prior to creation.

Nu/Ny/Nun is the "Subjective Being"; the symbol of the unformed, undefined, undifferentiated energy/matter, inert or inactive; the uncreated state before the creation. It cannot be the cause of its transformation.

The term "infinite", of course, is synonymous with "not finite", undefined, unlimited, unshaped, undifferentiated, and so on. This means that the energy/matter out of which all things are formed must be, in its essential state, unformed, undefined, undifferentiated, etc. If the material basis of the world had any essential definitions (formations), these would act as limiting factors to its ability to be transformed infinitely. Its essential lack of definition is an absolute requirement for God's creative omnipotence.

2.2 LET CREATION BEGIN—THE BIG BANG

The condensed energy in the pre-creation neutron soup was continuously building up. This condensed energy reached the optimum concentration of buildup energy that led to its explosion and expansion outwardly, in what we describe as the Big Bang, about 15 billion years ago.

The Big Bang was the first physical act of creation. The loud sound of this explosion is what caused the breakup of the constituent parts of the universe.

The Ancient Egyptian texts likewise repeatedly stressed that the divine commanding voice—meaning the Divine Sound – was the cause of creation.

The earliest recovered Ancient Egyptian texts 5,000 years ago show the belief that the Word caused the creation of the World. The Egyptian *Book of the Coming Forth by Light* (wrongly and commonly translated as the *Book of the Dead*), the oldest written text in the world, states:

> *"I am the Eternal ... I am that which created the Word ... I am the Word ..."*

2.3 ATAM—THE MANIFESTED COSMIC ENERGY

Creation came out of the state of no-creation. The Egyptians called it *Nun*. *None* or *nil* also represents the pre-creation state of the universe. There is NO universe: NONE NILL ZERO. Such a state of the universe represents the Subjective Being—unformed, undefined, and undifferentiated energy/matter. Its inert energy is inactive. On the other hand, the creation state is orderly, formed, defined, and differentiated. The totality of the divine energy during the creation state is called A-tam by the Egyptians.

A-Tam means the One-ness of all; the complete. It is connected with the root 'tam' or *'tamam'*, meaning *"to be complete"* or *"to make an end of"*.

In Ancient Egyptian texts, Atam/Atum means 'he who completes or perfects', and in the Litany of Re (Ra), Atam/Atum is recognized as **the Complete One; the ALL.**

The Ancient Egyptian texts emphasize that *'the complete one'* contains all. The Ancient Egyptian text reads:

> *"I am many of names and many of forms, and my Being exists in every neter (god, goddess)".*

The seed of creation—out of which everything originated – is Atam. And just as the plant is contained within the seed; so everything that is created in the universe is Atam, too.

Atam, **the One who is the All**, as the Master of the Universe, declares, in the Ancient Egyptian papyrus commonly known as the *Bremner-Rhind Papyrus:*

> *"When I manifested myself into existence, existence existed.*
> *I came into existence in the form of the Existent, which came into existence in the First Time.*
> *Coming into existence according to the mode of existence of the Existent, I therefore existed.*
> *And it was thus that the Existent came into existence".*

In other words, when the Master of the Universe came into existence, the whole creation came into existence, because the Complete One contains the all.

2.4 NETERU—THE DIVINE ENERGIES

As stated above, the Ancient Egyptian texts emphasize that the complete one contains all. The Ancient Egyptian text reads:

> *"I am many of names and many of forms, and my Being exists in every neter".*

The cycle of creation is caused and maintained by the divine forces or energies. These energies, like the perpetual cycle of creation, go through a process of transformation, from birth—life—aging—dying—death and rebirth. We, as human beings, have similar life forces that change throughout our lifetimes. Our human bodies consist of numerous cycles that govern our life existence. All forces die out when we die.

The Egyptians called these divine forces 'neteru'. The main theme of the universe is its cyclical nature. The NeTeRu are the forces of NaTuRe, which make the world go around—so to speak. To simply call them *gods* and *goddesses* gives a false impression.

The Divine energy that manifests itself in the creation cycle is defined by its constituent energy aspects, which were called neteru by the Ancient Egyptians. In order for creation to exist and to be maintained, this divine energy must be thought of in terms of male and female principles. Therefore, Ancient Egyptians expressed the cosmic energy forces in the terms of netert (female principle) and neter (male principle).

The Egyptian word neter or *nature* or *netjer* means *a power that is able to generate life and to maintain it when generated*. As all parts of creation go through the cycle of birth-life-death-rebirth, so do the driving energies, during the stages of this cycle. It is therefore that the Ancient Egyptian neteru, being divine energies, went (and continue to go) through the same cycle of birth-growth-death and renewal. Such understanding was common to all, as noted by Plutarch: that the multitude forces of nature known as neteru are born or created, are subject to continuous changes, age and die, and are reborn.

We can give the example of the caterpillar that is born, lives, then builds its own cocoon, where it dies – or better yet, transforms into a butterfly who lays eggs and on and on. What we have here is the cyclical transformation from one form/state of energy to another.

Another example is the water cycle—the water evaporates, forming clouds that rains back to earth. It is all an orderly cyclical transformation of energies in various forms.

When you think of neteru not as *gods* and *goddesses*. but as cosmic energy forces, one can see the Ancient Egyptian system as a brilliant representation of the universe. Philosophically, this cyclical natural transformation is applicable to our saying:

"The more things change, the more they stay the same".

In scientific circles, this is known as the natural law of conservation of energy, which is described as: **the principle that energy is never consumed but only changes form, and that the total energy in a physical system, such as the universe, cannot be increased or diminished.**

2.5 THE ENERGY MATRIX OF CREATION

This matrix of energies came as a result of the initial act of creation and the subsequent effects of the Big Bang that created the universe. This matrix consists of an organized hierarchy. Each level of the hierarchy of existence is a theophany—a creation by the consciousness of the level of being above it. The self-contemplation by each stage of existence brings into being each lower stage. As such, the hierarchy of energies is interrelated, and each level is sustained by the level below it. This hierarchy of energies is set neatly into a vast matrix of deeply interfaced natural laws. It is both physical and metaphysical.

The Ancient and Baladi Egyptians made/make no distinction between a metaphysical state of being and one with a material body. Such a distinction is a mental illusion. **We exist on a number of different levels at once, from the most physical to the most metaphysical.** Einstein agreed with the same principles.

Since Einstein's relativity theory, it has been known and accepted that matter is a form of energy; a coagulation or condensation of energy. As a result, the natural law for the conservation of matter or mass similarly states that matter is neither created nor destroyed during any physical or chemical change.

Energy is made up of molecules rotating or vibrating at various rates of speed. In the "physical" world, molecules rotate at a very slow and constant rate of speed. That is why things appear to be solid, to our earthly senses. The slower the speed, the more dense or solid the thing. In the metaphysical (spirit) world, the molecules vibrate at a much faster or ethereal dimension, where things are freer and less dense.

In this light, the universe is basically a hierarchy of energies at different orders of density. Our senses have some access to the densest form of energy, which is matter. The hierarchy of energies is interrelated, and each level is sustained by the level below it. This hierarchy of energies is set neatly into a vast matrix of deeply interfaced natural laws. It is both physical and metaphysical.

The universal energy matrix encompasses the world as a product of a complex system of relationships among people (living and dead), animals, plants, and natural and supernatural phenomena. This rationale is often called *Animism* because of its central premise that all things are animated (energized) by life forces. Each minute particle of everything is in constant motion, i.e. energized, as acknowledged in **the kinetic theory**. In other words, everything is animated (energized)—animals, trees, rocks, birds, even the air, sun, and moon.

The faster form of energies—these invisible energies in the universe—are called *spirits* by many. Spirits/energies are organized at different orders of densities, which relates to the different speeds of molecules. These faster (invisible) energies inhabit certain areas or are associated with particular natural phenomena. Spirits (energies) exist in family-type groups (i.e., related to each other).

Energies may occupy, at will, a more condensed energy (matter) such as human, animal, plant, or any form. The spirit animates the human body at birth and leaves it at death. Sometimes more than one energy spirit enters a body.

We often hear a person is 'not feeling himself/herself', who is 'temporarily insane', 'possessed', 'beside oneself'; or one who has multiple personalities. The energies (spirits) have an effect on all of us, to one degree or another.

The presence of energy in everything was long recognized by the Ancient and Baladi Egyptians. That there are cosmic energies (neteru) in every stone, mineral, wood, etc., is stated clearly in the **Shabaka Stele** (8th Century BCE):

> *"**And so the neteru** (gods, goddesses)entered into their*

bodies, in the form of every sort of wood, of every sort of mineral, as every sort of clay, as everything which grows upon him (meaning earth)".

2.6 CONFUSING NETERU WITH OTHER INVISIBLE ENTITIES

A major confusion exists in Western minds about the various invisible forces in the universe in the Egyptian system. They lumped them altogether as 'gods' and then gave them different ranks such as a major/minor/demon/genies/. This is amazing because all earlier writers of antiquities—such as Diodorus of Sicily, Plutarch, etc.—distinguished clearly the various forms of invisible beings in the Egyptian system. Basically, the Neteru [gods, goddesses] belong to the 'Upper Heavenly Court' while the other invisible powers that related to earthly activities belong to the 'Lower Heavenly Court'. More details will follow in a later chapter.

2.7 NETERU AND ANGELS

The neteru (gods, goddesses) are the representations of the energies/powers/forces, through their actions and interactions created, maintained, and continue to maintain the universe.

The neteru and their functions were later acknowledged by others as *angels*. The Song of Moses in *Deuteronomy* (32:43), as found in a cave at Qumran near the Dead Sea, mentions the word 'gods' in the plural:

"Rejoice, O heavens, with him; and do obeisance to him, ye gods". When the passage is quoted in the *New Testa-*

ment (Hebrews, 1:6), the word *gods* is substituted with *'angels of God'*.

The spheres of neteru (known also as angels and archangels in Christianity) are hierarchical among the levels/realms of the universe.

CHAPTER 3 : MANIFESTATION OF NETERU IN THE ORDERLY CREATION PROCESS

3.1 EGYPTIAN CREATION PROCESS ACCOUNTS

The origin of the world and the nature of the neteru [gods, goddesses] who took part in its creation were subjects of constant interest to the Egyptians.

Ancient Egyptians had four main cosmological teaching centers at Heliopolis , Memphis, Thebes, and Hermopolis. Each center revealed one of the principle phases or aspects of genesis. As such, creation accounts associated with the four centers are all consistent with the orderly formation of/within the universal energy matrix.

The system of creation is a system of necessary emanation, procession, or irradiation accompanied by necessary aspiration or reversion-to-source: all the forms and phases of Existence flow from the Divinity, and all strive to return thither and to remain there.

The main theme of all Ancient Egyptian texts is the perpetual cyclical of creation. Creation is not static. Creation is basically a process that follows a basic cycle of birth—life—death and rebirth. We recognize this cosmic cycle as the Big Bang, followed by life followed by the Big Crunch; then we are ready again for a big bounce and a new creation cycle. Not only that, but the whole universe follows this cycle – man and other creatures follow this basic cycle on various scales, as well.

[More details about the creation process from various and complimentary ways are to be found in the book *Egyptian Cosmology: The Animated Universe* by Moustafa Gadalla.]

3.2 THE THREE PRIMARY PHASES OF THE CREATION CYCLE

The division into three parts is a dominant feature of any cycle. The sequence of the creation cycle is delineated into three primary phases in the Ancient Egyptian texts. The very same delineations were later on duplicated in Sufi (and other) teachings.

The following are three main Ancient Egyptian sources for such triple delineations:

A. Pyramid Texts: Consistent with the theme of three phases of the creation cycle, we find that, as far back as at least 5000 years ago, the Pyramid Texts reveals the existence of three companies of neteru (gods, goddesses), and each company consisted of 9 neteru (gods, goddesses). Throughout the Pyramid Texts, frequent mention is made of one group or of 2 or 3 groups of 9 neteru (gods, goddesses).

The Egyptian texts speak of three Enneads, each representing a phase in the creation cycle.

The first (Great) Ennead represents the conceptual or divine stage. This is governed by Re (Ra).

The second Ennead represents the manifestation stage. This is governed by Osiris.

The third Ennead represents the return to the Source, combining both Re and Osiris.

In *The Book of the Coming Forth By Light*, both the souls of Osiris and Re meet and are united to form an entity, described so eloquently:

> *I am His Two Souls in his Twins.*

Nine is the number of each phase—and each phase begets the following phase in 9 terms.

B. Litany of Re (Ra): After a brief preface, the Litany opens with seventy-five invocations to the Forms of Re, followed by a series of prayers and hymns in which the roles of Re and Osiris are constantly stressed.

The perpetual cycle of Osiris and Re dominates the text in its three phases. The first phase is the manifestation of Re in his forms. The second phase is the manifestation of Aus-Re [Osiris] in his forms. The third and final phase occurs in the Netherlands, where both Osiris and Re join together and resurrect as a new *Horus Herakhuti of the Two Horizons* [more details throughout this book, in later chapters].

C. Leiden Papyrus J350: This surviving Ancient Egyptian document is dated to at least since the Old Kingdom

(2575–2150 BCE); a copy of which was reproduced during the reign of Ramses II in the 13th century BCE.

The Leiden Papyrus J350 consists of an extended composition, describing the principle aspects of the ancient creation narratives. The system of numeration in the Papyrus identifies the principle/aspect of creation and matches each one with its symbolic number. The manuscript is divided into a series of numbered "stanzas". Each is entitled "Mansions [of the moon], number xx".

The numbering system of this Egyptian Papyrus by itself is significant. They are numbered in three tiers—1 to 9, and then the powers 10, 20, 30, to 90 to constitute the energetic foundations of physical forms—and the third tier are numbered in the 100s.

This numbering system shows the three phases of the creation cycle as being:

1. The Conceiving Phase/Ennead whose theme is the objectification of a circumscribed area of undifferentiated energy/matter wherein the world will be manifested. It consists of the establishment of order and the co-factors of life-forms as the foundation for the world. Phase One consists basically of three consecutive groups; each of which consists of 3 stages.

2. The Orderly Manifestation Phase/Ennead deals with the creation of the noumenal and phenomenal planes—the two grand subdivisions of the manifested world.

3. The Reunification Phase/Ennead, whose theme is

the return to the Source and subsequent reunification process that leads to a NEW Alpha.

[For the details of the three phases of creation cycle, see *Egyptian Alphabetical Letters of Creation Cycle* by Moustafa Gadalla.]

3.3 THE ARCHETYPAL SOLAR CYCLE

The most obvious and universal cycle, to humans, is the solar cycle. The Egyptian model depiction of the solar cycle is represented by the Egyptian netert [goddess] Nut, as the Firmament. The sun voyages the body of Nut from sunrise to sunrise. The sun—born anew each morning – crosses the sky in the solar bark, ages, dies and travels through the underworld during the night in a cycle of regeneration.

The human being goes through a similar cycle. One goes through the cycle of Birth—Life—Death—Resurrection. The Ancient Egyptian transformational (funerary) texts always make reference to this similarity, and illustrate the concept that Resurrection will follow Death and a new cycle will start—an everlasting new life.

Ground zero of the cycle was/is the crucial moment of sunrise. The Ancient Egyptians were fascinated by this point of beginning.

The baboon represents this point of beginning extremely well. The baboon is almost human and as such, it represents this crucial moment that precedes the awakening of the sun. The baboon represents this state in humans, just before they gain consciousness—the awakening.

CHAPTER 4 : UNDERSTANDING NAMES, EPITHETS & TITLES

4.1 THE REAL SECRET NAMES

As stated earlier, Egyptian creation texts repeatedly stress the belief of creation by the Word. We find that in the *Book of the Divine Cow* (found in the shrines of Tut-AnkhAmen), Re (Ra) creates the heavens and its hosts merely by pronouncing some words whose sound alone evokes the names of things—and these things then appear at his bidding. As its name is pronounced, so the thing comes into being, for the name is a reality; the thing itself.

In Egyptian belief, names express the fundamental nature of the things to which they refer. The neteru's (gods, goddesses) real names were kept secret, since they conveyed their true natures and powers. To know the true name of a deity was to have power over it. The importance of names is demonstrated by the Egyptian allegory of *the Mystery of the Divine Name*, found on an Ancient Egyptian papyrus now in the Turin Museum. In this allegory, Re refused to tell even the most beloved Being, Isis, his real (secret) name. The events of the story end with Re "divulging" his "secret" name as *Amen*. It should be noted that *Amen* means *secret/hidden*. In other words, under all difficult circumstances, Re (as a model for all) did not divulge his real name, but only stated that his secret name was [Amen] secret.

The role of the name in Ancient and Baladi Egypt was not, as per our modern-day thinking, a mere label. The name of a neter, person, animal, or principle represents a resume or synopsis of the qualities of that person or object. The real name was/is imbued with magical powers and properties. To know and pronounce the real name of a neter (god, goddess), man, or animal is to exercise power over it.

The learned and most trusted people in an Egyptian community knew/know the great real (or secret) names of the neteru (gods, goddesses) and other cosmic forces, and used this knowledge to maintain order in the world.

The real names of the deities (gods, goddesses) were kept secret so as to guard the cosmic power of the deity.

4.2 THEIR EPITHETS

In keeping with this belief, deities are recognized by their roles. The neteru were referred to by epithets that describe particular qualities, attributes and/or aspect(s) of their roles. Because of the neteru's (gods, goddesses) multiple and overlapping roles, deities can have many epithets.

This is similar to a person who is an engineer at work, a father at home, a coach in the field, a military reservist at weekends and emergencies, etc.

Here are a few examples of Egyptian epithets of neteru

[gods, goddesses] that were cavalierly called "names" by academicians:

• Nun, which is pronounced as 'none,' is a word that means 'nothing/nothingness', which is the exact description of what uninformed people considered as a 'deity'.

• Earlier we talked about the significance of the word/name Atam/Atum/Atem, which means *complete*.

• The netert (goddess) Sekhmet is actually two words, Sekh and -Mut, meaning *Elder Mother* or *Den Mother,* with all the qualities of a Den Mother.

• Amen/Amun means "hidden one".

• The neter [god] Ausar [commonly recognized as Osiris'] actually consists of two words—*Aus* and *Ra*.

The word **Aus** means ***the power of***, or ***the root of***. As such, the name Ausar consists of two parts: Aus-Ra, meaning *the power of Ra*, meaning the re-birth of Ra (Re).

The principle that makes life come from apparent death was/is called Ausar, who symbolizes the power of renewal. Ausar represents the process, growth, and underlying cyclical aspects of the universe. The main theme of the Ancient Egyptian texts is the cyclical nature of creation being born, living, dying, and regenerating again.

• As a follow-up to the meaning of Aus in the epithet

Aus-ra (Osiris), we follow with the feminine form of the word 'Aus'. In Semitic languages (following the Egyptian system), two genders, masculine and feminine, are distinguished for nouns, adjectives, and also verbs. The feminine forms are regularly derived from the masculine by adding the suffix at/et at the end of the word, for singular form. As such, the feminine form of Aus (meaning source/ origin/basis) is Aus-et, which is the Egyptian name for Isis.

Later on, the significance of the etymology of other epithets [so-called "names"] will be explained in later chapters.

4.3 CONSEQUENCES OF IGNORING THE PRINCIPLES OF EGYPTIAN LANGUAGE

In most (or practically all) references about Ancient Egypt, writers dealt with Egyptian epithets with a total disregard for the intent and nature of the Egyptian language. Epithets and the like must be understood in the context of the Egyptian language.

Present popularized 'names' of deities suffer from three main ignorances of certain facts in the Egyptian language. They are:

1. Arbitrary additions of vowel sounds so as to help Western tongues pronounce Egyptian words.

As in all Semitic styles of writings, Ancient Egyptian writing was limited to the consonants of the words. In all these languages, the meaning of the word is generally contained in the consonants while unwritten/implicit vowels indicate the grammatical forms. For people (even at the present time) who are brought up in Semitic language-speaking countries, it is very easy to figure out the pronunciation of any word (without notating vowels and other phonetic marks), based on the context or a syntactical feature. As an example: the name Mohammed is spelled in four Arabic letters, and is written (even in our present time) as such—MHMD. Any Arabic-speaking person has no problem vocalizing MHMD even without [explicit] vowels and/or phonetic marks.

The Western disregard for the [unwritten] vocalization led to ending up with variations in writing the same Ancient Egyptian term, such as Amen/Amon/Amun or Aton/Aten. This is because the vowels you see in translated Egyptian texts are only approximations of sounds which are used by Western Egyptologists to help them pronounce Ancient Egyptian terms/words.

2. They disregarded words' separation, and as a result, they combined two/three words in a single word—such as Sekhmet, as explained above.

3. They chose one [of many] grammatical variations and called it a "name". For the sake of "simplification", they destroyed the intent/meaning and killed the subject in the process. The question is, then, why there are writing variations for an epithet.

Ancient Egyptian (and Semitic) grammar distinguishes three parts of speech: nouns, verbs, and particles. What would be called adjectives, adverbs, and pronouns in other languages are considered nouns in the Egyptian Semitic language family. In its purest Ancient Egyptian form, all nouns can be easily derived from the root verb

(verb-stem) which consists of three consonants, which are called radicals.

Words are formed from roots by the addition of (unwritten) vowels, prefixes, infixes, or suffixes according to certain fixed patterns that correspond to grammatical rules. Such is the reason for having variations in writing epithets in Ancient Egyptian records. [More about the language in Ancient Egypt in other books by Moustafa Gadalla, as shown at the end of this book.]

4.4 SPEAKING OF TITLES

The Ancient Egyptians also used generic words that were also confused by foreign academicians as "names", while in reality they are simple words with religious connotations. *Baal* simply means *Lord* or *ruler*, and so we hear of the *Baal* or the *Baalat* (Lady) of such-and-such a city. Similarly, a deity will be called *Melek*, meaning *King*. So, too *Adon*; which means *Lord* or *Master*. *Melqart* meant *King* of the City. Other "names" meaning favored/ granted by the neteru (gods, goddesses) are recognized as *Fortunatus, Felix, Donatus, Concessus*, and so on.

CHAPTER 5 : NARRATION OF THEIR MANIFESTATIONS

The totality of the Egyptian civilization was built upon a complete and precise understanding of universal laws. This profound understanding manifested itself in a consistent, coherent and interrelated system, where art, science, philosophy and religion were intertwined and were employed simultaneously in a single organic Unity.

Egyptian cosmology is based on coherent scientific and philosophical principles. The cosmological knowledge of Ancient Egypt was expressed in story form, which is a superior means for expressing both physical and metaphysical concepts. Any good writer or lecturer knows that stories are better than exposition for explaining the behavior of things because the relationships of parts to each other, and to the whole, are better maintained by the mind. Information alone is useless unless it is transformed into understanding.

The Egyptian sagas transformed common factual nouns and adjectives (indicators of qualities) into proper but conceptual nouns. These were, in addition, personified so that they could be woven into coherent and meaningful narratives. Personification is based on their knowledge that man was made in the image of God and, as such, represented the created image of all creation.

Allegories are an intentionally chosen means for communicating knowledge. Allegories dramatize cosmic laws, principles, processes, relationships, and functions, and express them in an easy-to-understand way. Once the inner meanings of the allegories have been revealed, they become marvels of simultaneous scientific and philosophical completeness and conciseness. The more they are studied, the richer they become. The 'inner dimension' of the teachings embedded into each story are capable of revealing several layers of knowledge, according to the stage of development of the listener. The "secrets" are revealed as one evolves higher. The higher we get, the more we see. It is always there.

The Egyptians (Ancient and present-day Baladi) did/do not believe their allegories as historical facts. They believed IN them, in the sense that they believed in the truth beneath the stories.

Throughout this book, several subjects will be explained in story forms, using four personified concepts: Isis,

Osiris, Horus, and Seth. Four of such subjects will be:

1. The solar and lunar principles as represented by Isis and Osiris.

2. The four elements of the world (water, fire, earth, and air), equated to Osiris, Seth, Isis and Horus, respectively.

3. The model societal framework is expressed in the legendary Allegory of Isis, Osiris, Horus and Seth.

4. Numerology and trigonometry, as well as the trinity/triad/triangle cosmic role, as described in the relationship between the father [Osiris], mother [Isis], and son [Horus], are analogous to the right angle triangle 3:4:5.

The Egyptian well-crafted mystery plays are an intentionally chosen means for communicating knowledge.

Meaning and the mystical experience are not tied to a literal interpretation of events. Once the inner meanings of the narratives have been revealed, they become marvels of simultaneous scientific and philosophical completeness and conciseness. The more they are studied, the richer they become. And, rooted in the narrative as it is, the part can never be mistaken for the whole; nor can its functional significance be forgotten or distorted.

CHAPTER 6 : COMMON MISREPRESENTATIONS OF THE DIVINITIES IN EGYPT

A neter/netert (god/goddess) may have contradictory aspects.

> "Contradictory aspects" can be interrelated. Take for example the aspect of motherhood as represented by a netert (goddess). A mother can be tender and can be ferocious, depending on the circumstances. These are not contradictory qualities. Normally, a mother will be tender to her child, but if her child is threatened, she becomes ferocious and will attack the outside threat.

A neter (god) may be represented in different forms or shapes.

> The nature of neter/netert (god/goddess) may vary under changing conditions. In human terms, the nature of water is present in different forms:

- as a vapor—in humid air.
- as a liquid—in rain.
- as a solid—in an ice cube.

There were always power struggles between the different

"cult centers."

> There were neither "political/religious struggles" nor "cult centers" in Ancient Egypt. Western academic Egyptologists who claim such nonsense are projecting the history of the church onto the Ancient Egyptian history.

The neteru (gods/goddesses) have complementary functions to each other. Since each neter/netert (god/goddess) represents a function, s/he can be found in any temple/tomb/text. A neter/netert may have a prominent (but never exclusive) role at any temple. All temples were of equal importance, and the Egyptian Pharaohs performed the ritual services throughout Egypt at all the temples.

The Egyptians gave a neter/netert (god/goddess) different names.

> Names in Ancient Egypt were not just labels. A name was like a short resume or synopsis of the principle. For example, the neter (god) Ra (Re) is described in the Unas Funerary (Pyramid) Texts:

> *"They cause thee to come into being as Re, in his name of Khepri."*

Khepri is not just another label/name for Re. Khepri means coming into being. Also see previous chapter: Understanding Names, Epithets & Titles.

Egypt went through an "evolution" of religious beliefs, where the nature of the neteru (gods/goddesses) changed over the centuries. They intermingled with outsiders' beliefs, assimilating some divinities (gods/goddesses), but also creating new ones.

> This is sheer nonsense, fabricated by Western academic

Egyptologists who ignore the facts of the times. ALL early historians of the Greek and Roman times confirmed that the Egyptians are remarkably traditionalist to a fault. For example, Herodotus (5th century BCE) stated in *The Histories–Book Two*, Section 79:

> *"The Egyptians keep to their native customs and never adopt any from abroad."*

In *Book Two*, Section 91, Herodotus states:

> *"The Egyptians are unwilling to adopt Greek customs, or, to speak generally, those of any other country."*

Herodotus, in the *Histories, Book Two* [2-8], wrote:

> *"The names of nearly all the gods came to Greece from Egypt".*

This makes sense once we recognize that replacing letters (sound shift) is a common worldwide phenomenon. From the earliest days of comparative philology, it was noticed that the sounds of related languages corresponded in apparently systematic ways. As an example of the phenomenon of sound shift, a person's name can still be recognized in vastly different sounds, such as Santiago/San Diego/San Jacob and Saint James. Jacob/Jack/Jaques/James are one and the same name, which exemplifies the phenomenon of sound shift.

It should be noted, as explained earlier, that what we commonly consider to be names of deities are actually their epithets or titles.

CHAPTER 7 : MAN AND THE DIVINE FORCES

7.1 MAN'S PLACE IN THE UNIVERSAL ORDER

As shown earlier, the universe is basically a hierarchy of energies at different orders of density. Our senses have some access to the densest form of energy, which is matter. The hierarchy of energies is interrelated, and each level is sustained by the level below it. This hierarchy of energies is set neatly into a vast matrix of deeply inter-faced natural laws. It is both physical and metaphysical.

The faster forms of energies—these invisible energies in the universe—are called spirits, by many. Spirits/energies are organized at different orders of densities, which relates to the different speeds of molecules. These faster (invisible) energies inhabit certain areas or are associated with particular natural phenomena. Spirits (energies) exist in family-type groups (i.e., related to each other).

Ancient and Baladi Egyptians believe that the universal energy matrix consists of the unity's inter-penetrating and interactive nine realms, which are commonly classified as seven heavens (metaphysical realms) and two earths (physical realms).

The two earthly realms are commonly known as The Two Lands. The number 8 is our physical (earthly) realm. The last realm—number 9—is where our complimentary opposite exists. [For more detailed information about this subject, read *Egyptian Cosmology: The Animated Universe* by Moustafa Gadalla.]

According to Egyptian philosophy, though all creation is spiritual in origin, man is born mortal but contains within himself the seed of the divine. His purpose in this life is to nourish that seed; and his reward, if successful, is eternal life, where he will reunite with his divine origin. Nourishing plants in the soil is analogous to nourishing the spirit on Earth by doing good deeds.

Man comes into the world with the higher divine faculties, which are the essence of his/her salvation, in an unawakened state. The way of Egyptian religion is, therefore, a system of practices aimed at awakening these dormant higher faculties. [For more detailed information about this subject, read *Egyptian Cosmology: The Animated Universe* by Moustafa Gadalla.]

7.2 THE IMAGE OF THE UNIVERSE

It is commonly recognized by all theological and philosophical schools of thought that the human being is made in the image of God – i.e., a miniature universe – and that to understand the universe is to understand oneself, and vice versa.

Yet, no culture has ever practiced the above principle like the Ancient Egyptians. Central to their complete understanding of the universe was the knowledge that man was the embodiment of the laws of creation. As such, the physiological functions and processes of the various parts of the body were seen as manifestations of cosmic functions.

The Ancient Egyptian texts and symbols are permeated with this complete understanding that man (in whole and part) is the image of the universe (whole and part).

To Ancient Egyptians, man, as a miniature universe, represents the created images of all creation. Since Re (Ra)—the cosmic creative impulse—is called *"The One Join together, Who Comes Out of His Own Members"*, so the human being (the image of creation) is, likewise, *A One Joined Together*. The human body is a unity that consists of different parts joined together. In the Litany of Re, the body parts of the divine man are each identified with a neter/netert.

If man is the universe in miniature, then all factors in man are duplicated on a greater scale in the universe. All drives and forces which are powerful in man are also powerful in the universe at large. In accordance with the Egyptians' cosmic consciousness, every action performed by man is believed to be linked to a greater pattern in the universe, including sneezing, blinking, spitting, shouting, weeping, dancing, playing, eating, drinking, and sexual intercourse.

Man, to the Ancient Egyptians, was the embodiment of the laws of creation. As such, the physiological functions and processes of various parts of the body were seen as manifestations of cosmic functions. Limbs and organs had a metaphysical function, in addition to their physical purpose. The parts of the body were consecrated to one of the neteru (divine principles), which appeared in the Egyptian records throughout its recovered history. In addition to the *Litany of Re*, here are other examples:

- Utterance 215 § 148-149, from the Sarcophagus Chamber of Unas' Tomb (rubble pyramid) at Saqqara, identifies the parts of the body (head, nose, teeth, arms, legs, etc.), each with the divine neteru:

  Thy head is that of Horus
  . . .
  thy nose is a Anubis
  thy teeth are Sopdu
  thy arms are Happy and Dua-mutef,
  . . .
  thy legs are Imesty and Kebeh-senuf,
  . . .
  All thy members are the twins of Atam.

- From the *Papyrus of Ani*, [pl. 32, item 42]:

  My hair is Nun; my face is Re; my eyes are Hathor; my ears are Wepwawet; my nose is She who presides over her lotus-leaf; my lips are Anubis; my molars are Selket; my incisors are Isis; my arms are the Ram, the Lord of Mendes; my breast is Neith; my back is Seth; my phallus is Osiris; . . . my belly and my spine are Sekhmet; my buttocks are the Eye of Horus; my thighs and my calves are Nut; my feet are Ptah; . . . there is no member of mine devoid of a neter (god), and Thoth is the protection of all my flesh.

The above text leaves no doubt about the divinity of each member: <u>*there is no member of mine devoid of a neter (god)*</u>.

The logical (and only) way to explain anything to human beings is on human terms and in human form. As such, the complicated scientific and philosophical information was reduced in Ancient Egypt, to events in human images and terms.

7.3 THE TWO HEAVENLY COURTS

The Egyptians made two broad distinctions in the hierarchical metaphysical structure of the seven heavenly realms, as follows:

> A. At the highest end of this celestial order, there exist three levels in a sort of heavenly court or council that are the equivalents of the Arch-angels and the Orders of Angels which we find in other systems of religion. Those are not involved with human activities on Earth

> B. The Egyptians distinguished four lower groups that occupy in the celestial hierarchy positions identical with those of some Oriental Christian systems, the prophets, apostles, martyrs, and many great saints. Those lived on Earth for one time or another and after their Earthly departure, they continue to be involved with human activities on Earth.

In all periods of Egyptian history there existed this class of beings, some of whom are male and some female. They had many forms and shapes and could appear on Earth as men, women, animals, birds, reptiles, trees, plants, etc. They were stronger and more intelligent than men, but they had passions like men. They were credited with possessing some divine powers or characteristics, and yet they could suffer sickness and die.

[More info about the interaction between beings/energies in the universe is found in *Egyptian Cosmology: The Animated Universe* by Moustafa Gadalla.]

7.4 THE THREE PRIMARY HEAVENLY HELPERS

These are what are erroneously described as *Minor Gods, Local Gods,* etc. They are not a part of the neteru (gods, goddesses), as indicated earlier. Such groups lived on earth for one time or another, and after their Earthly departure, they continue to be involved with human activities on Earth, and are generally divided into three groups:

i. Family and close relatives

ii. Community Patrons—[Ancestral local/regional patrons]

The character of such departed souls as community patrons ["local gods"] cover a broad range, fulfilling the expectations of their descendants in the community at large.

They behave like superior human beings with the same passions and the same needs; but also with transcendental power. The city is the "House" of the 'patron'.

They have shrines, holy objects and statues. They may appear in the form of stones, trees, animals or human beings.

It is conceivable that the patron of a particularly great

and mighty town should be believed to exercise a sort of patronage, either politically or agriculturally, over that part which he had attained. This would determine his expanding influence on a larger area position, and he would become a great patron with a wider regional area.

Certain shrines show them to be purely local 'patrons; many originally named after the towns; such as "him of Ombos", "him of Edfu", or "her of Bast" – they are really merely the genii of the towns.

iii. Folk Saints

Walis (folk saints) are the people who succeeded in traveling the spiritual Path, and who have attained union with the Divine. Such unification enables them to perform supernatural acts, influence and predict future events, etc. As a result, they become the intermediaries between the earthly living beings and the supernatural, heavenly realms.

After their earthly deaths, their spiritual force/blessing is thought to increase and to inhere in the persons (and, particularly, the places) associated with and chosen by them. [More information about such heavenly helpers and interactions with them can be found in *Egyptian Cosmology: The Animated Universe* and *Egyptian Mystics: Seekers of The Way;* both publications by Moustafa Gadalla.]

7.5 EGYPTIAN TEMPLES OF THE DIVINE FORCES

The Egyptian temple is the link, the proportional mean, between the Macro-cosmos (world) and Micro-cosmos (man). It was a stage on which meetings were enacted between the neter (god) and the king, as representative of the people. It was the place in which the cosmic energy, neter (god) came to dwell and radiate its energy to the land and people.

It is therefore that the Egyptian temple was not a place of public worship—in our "modern" understanding. It was the interface between the divine forces and humans. The Egyptian temple served as the theater in which symbolic rituals were performed by the Pharaoh and his designated priests providing assurances that the society has confirmed to its divine obligations of hard work, virtues, justice, harmony and order. In return, the divine forces [Neteru] gave acceptance, prosperity, etc. In short the Egyptian temple was the source of power by which all of the Egyptian society followed.

These truly divine places were accessible only to the priesthood, who could enter the inner sanctuaries, where the sacred rites and ceremonies were performed. In some instances, only the King himself or his authorized substitute had permission to enter.

[For information about all religious aspects on all levels see *Egyptian Cosmology: The Animated Universe*; *Egyptian Mystics: Seekers of The Way* and *The Ancient Egyptian Metaphysical Architecture*; all these publications authored by by Moustafa Gadalla.]

PART II : THE ROLES OF MOST RECOGNIZED NETERU (GODS/GODDESSES)

CHAPTER 8 : MYSTICAL PICTORIAL DEPICTIONS

8.1 PICTORIAL SYMBOLISM OF THE NETERU

The metaphorical and symbolic presentation of depicted neteru (gods, goddesses) on the Egyptian monuments and documents was unanimously acknowledged by all early writers on the subject, such as Plutarch, Diodorus, Plotinus, Clement, etc.

A symbol, by definition, is not what it represents, but what it stands for, what it suggests. A symbol reveals to the mind a reality other than itself. Words convey information; symbols evoke understanding.

Each pictorial symbol is worth a thousand words—representing that function or principle, on all levels simultaneously—from the simplest, most obvious physical manifestation of that function to the most abstract and metaphysical. This symbolic language represents a wealth of physical, physiological, psychological and spiritual data in the presented symbols.

>>> It should be noted that the digital edition of this book as published in PDF and E-book formats has a

substantial number of photographs that compliment the text materials throughout this chapter.

8.2 HOW DO EGYPTIAN DEPICTIONS REFLECT METAPHYSICAL CONCEPTS?

We will show here the four main components of such Egyptian metaphysical depictions:

1. Man depiction signifies The Universe—Earthly and Divine
2. Animal Symbolism
3. Accessories, Emblems, color, etc.
4. Action forms

1. Man depiction signifies The Universe—Earthly and Divine

So many phrases are being used throughout the world which consistently state that the human being is made in the image of God (i.e. a miniature universe); and that to understand the universe is to understand oneself, and vice versa.

Yet, no culture has ever practiced the above principle like the Ancient Egyptians. Central to their complete understanding of the universe was the knowledge that man was made in the image of God and, as such, man represented the image of all creation.

Consistent with such thinking, a depicted human being represents both the universe as a whole as well as the human being on Earth.

According to Egyptian philosophy, though all creation is

spiritual in origin, man is born mortal but contains within himself the seed of the divine. His purpose in this life is to nourish that seed, and his reward, if successful, is eternal life, where he will reunite with his divine origin.

Egyptian artwork clearly depicted the earthly man and the progression to ultimately become one with the Divine.

Egyptian figuration carefully mark—with a headband, crown, diadem, or joint—a dividing line for the top of the skull of the earthly man, thus separating the crown of the skull. The height of the body was measured exclusive of the crown. The illustrations show the earthly man as always higher than the divine aspects. A clear example is found here in this Ancient Egyptian papyrus with a grid system, where a human is higher than the neter (god) Thoth.

The difference in the height between the two realms reflects the Ancient Egyptian deep understanding of the physiology and role of humans on earth. The removal of this part of the human brain leaves man alive, but without discernment – hence, with no personal judgment. The person is in a vegetated state; i.e. living and acting only as the executant of an impulse that he receives, without actual choice. It is like a person in a coma.

The earthly being must use his cerebral instrument to choose his actions. These actions will be in agreement or at variance with natural harmony. If, during his/her earthly life, the actions are not harmonious with nature, s/he will reincarnate again to the earthly realm, to try another time.

2. Animal Symbolism

The Egyptians' careful observation and profound knowledge of the natural world enabled them to identify certain animals with specific qualities that could symbolize certain divine functions and principles in a particularly pure and striking fashion.

As such, certain animals were chosen as symbols for that particular aspect of divinity.

This effective mode of expression is consistent with all cultures. For example, in the West they use expressions such as: *quiet as a mouse, sly like a fox*, etc.

When we talk about loyalty, there is no better way to express loyalty than a dog.

When we talk about the protective aspect of motherhood, there is no better way to express it than a lioness.

This symbolic expression of deep spiritual understanding was presented in three main forms. The first and second are animal-headed humans or a pure animal form, as we see below in an example for the dog Anubis.

The animal or animal-headed neteru (gods/goddesses) are symbolic expressions of a deep spiritual understanding. When a total animal is depicted in Ancient Egypt, it represents a particular function/attribute in its purest form. When an animal-headed figure is depicted, it conveys that particular function/attribute in the human being. The two forms of Anubis, in the two illustrations shown here, clearly distinguish these two aspects.

The third form is the opposite of an animal-headed human.

In this case, we have a human-headed bird—that is, the Ba—representing the body's soul, hovering over the body. The depiction of the Ba then is the divine aspect of the terrestrial.

The Ba is depicted as a stork. The stork is known for its

migrating and homing instinct, and is also known worldwide as the bird that carries newborn babies to their new families. The stork returns to its own nest with consistent precision—hence, a migratory bird is the perfect choice to represent the soul.

3. Accessories, Emblems, Color, etc.

In Egyptian symbolism, the precise role of the neteru (gods/goddesses) is revealed in many ways: by dress, headdress, crown, feather, animal, plant, color, position, size, gesture, sacred object (e.g., flail, scepter, staff, ankh), etc. This symbolic language represents a wealth of physical, physiological, psychological and spiritual data in the presented symbols.

A headdress identifies the deity and its particular function or functions. The depiction below of a seat identifies Isis as the legitimate source of authority.

Maat is identified by the feather of truth mounted on her head.

Several other examples are shown throughout this book.

4. Action Forms

Practically all figures on the walls of Egyptian monuments are in profile form, indicative of action and interaction between the various symbolic figures. A wide variety of actions are evident in the forms.

The pictorial depiction both in hieroglyphs and figurative images are presented in animated, precise, active modes.

The Egyptians proportioned the pictorial figures, as well as the hieroglyphs, by the application of generative dynamic design [more details in *Ancient Egyptian Metaphysical Architecture* by Moustafa Gadalla].

[For detailed information about the scientific/metaphysical realities of pictorial images, see *The Egyptian Hieroglyphic Metaphysical Language* by Moustafa Gadalla.]

CHAPTER 9 : MOST COMMON ANIMALS AND BIRDS FORMS DIVINITIES

The metaphysical significance of animal images is the subject of this chapter. The primary function of these Egyptian ideograms is to represent thoughts. This means that one must be searching for both the Figurative (an object stands for one of its qualities) and the Allegorical (an object is linked through enigmatic conceptual processes).

We must always keep in mind the relationship between visual forms and their meaning. A visual form may be mimetic or imitative, directly copying features of the object it represents; it may be associative, suggesting attributes which are not visually present such as abstract properties incapable of literal depiction; and finally, it may be symbolic, meaningful only when decoded according to conventions or systems of knowledge which, though not inherently visual, are communicated through visual means.

The Egyptians' careful observation and profound knowledge of the natural world enabled them to identify certain animals with specific qualities that could symbolize certain divine functions and principles in a particularly pure and striking fashion. As such, certain animals were chosen as symbols for that particular aspect of divinity. The more we learn about these animals' nature, characteristics, attributes, behavior, etc., the more we realize/recognize the meaning's possibilities.

In this chapter, we will show the most common animals and bird forms for the Egyptian divinities/neteru, with a very brief review of each's metaphysical functions/attributes to help stay away from silly descriptions and focus on the REAL subtle/deep meanings. It is always helpful to think of 'figures of speech' related to each image to recognize each's nature/behavior/characteristics/attributes. Such animals and birds are arranged here in alphabetical order.

>>> **It should be noted that the digital edition of this book as published in PDF and E-book formats has a substantial number of photographs that compliment the text materials throughout this chapter.**

— — — — —

Ass

Various attributes are all related to the ass. The specific attribute will be determined in the context being either 'good' or 'evil'. Here we will deal with one of its primary attributes, being the Ego.

Controlling the ego was/is one of the most important ethical requirements in Ancient and Baladi Egypt. One must know how to control it by riding the ass—the ego. Egyptian scenes (such as the one shown below) and texts provide the ass analogy that resonated later in the following biblical verses which describe the same concept of being humble and controlling the ego:

> *"Behold, your king is coming to you, humble, and mounted on an ass, and on a colt, the foal of an ass."*
> [Matthew, 21:5]

One of the Egyptian King's titles was *The Most Humble*. His abode while on Earth was made of mud-brick, the same material used by the humblest peasants.

The symbolic Ancient Egyptian scene here shows Horus and his four disciples, each armed with a knife, demonstrating to Osiris their success in controlling the ego.

Their success is symbolized by the ass-headed man (the symbol of the ego in man) with knives stuck in his body, bound by his arms to the forked stick.

Baboon

The baboon represents the starting point of a Cycle (a creation cycle or a daily cycle).

The baboon represents this point of beginning extremely well. The baboon is almost human; and as such, it represents this crucial moment that precedes the awakening of the sun.

The baboon emits a crackling sound at the crack of dawn, The Point of beginning.

In such role, the baboon is associated with Thoth [Tehuti]—the divine intermediary between the metaphysical (the darkness before dusk) and the Physical (as the light is coming forth).

In Ancient Egyptian traditions, the words of Re (Ra), revealed through Thoth (Hermes, Mercury), became the things and creatures of this world; i.e. the words (meaning sound energies) created the forms in the universe. As such, Thoth represents the link between the metaphysical (extra-human) and the physical (terrestrial). Such a link by Thoth represents the crack of dawn, and therefore Thoth is related to the baboon.

The baboon is usually depicted as sitting, waiting for Moment Zero,

or standing up, hailing the coming of a new cycle.

Consistent with the baboon's role, we find that one of the four Disciples of Horus is baboon-headed. His role is to watch over the Eastern quadrant—the region where new/renewed creation comes forth.

— — — — —

Beetle

Re is frequently represented as a large black scarab beetle sitting in the solar boat and rolling the sun disc; or as a man whose human head is replaced by a scarab beetle.

As such, Re is the original divine scarab. The Egyptian

name for the scarab beetle was Khepri, a multiple word meaning:

"This who brings into being."

Re (Ra) is described in the *Unas Funerary (Pyramid) Texts*:

"They cause thee to come into being as Re, in the name of Khepri".

Khepri the scarab beetle is one of the 75 Manifestation of the creation process—all being aspects of Re, the divine creative force.

Horapollo Niliaeus explains the symbolism of the scarab in this way:

"To signify the only begotten, or birth, or a father, or the world, or man, they [Egyptians] draw a scarab. The only begotten, because this animal is self-begotten, unborn of the female. For its birth takes place only in the following way. When the male wishes to have off-spring, it takes some cow-dung and makes a round ball of it, very much in the shape of the world. Rolling it with its hind legs from east to west, it faces the east, so as to give it the shape of the world, for the world is borne from the east to the west."

In the Ancient Egyptian transformational (funerary) texts, the deceased, identified with Osiris, passed through analogous stages in the night of the underworld and was reborn as a new Ra (Re) in his form of Khepri (the scarab beetle) in the morning. The analogy to the sun—disappearing at night and appearing in the morning—is clear. The scarab is the symbol of the transforming quality of the sun; the light that comes out of darkness. Scarab amulets were customarily buried with the deceased to promote rebirth.

The scarab beetle is, therefore, always found at the beginning of a cycle.

———————

Bennu/Benben

Bennu is represented as a flying bird—as a composite heron and stork, or as a composite of the falcon and stork.

The stork is known for its migrating and homing instinct, and is also known worldwide as the bird that carries newborn babies to their new families.

Bennu, in the form of stork, brings a New Life.

The stork returns to its own nest with consistent precision—hence, a migratory bird is the perfect choice to represent the soul returning to the Source.

At the Source, Bennu is depicted perched on Benben, the symbol of the primeval hill.

In this regard, Bennu is the Phoenix rising from the ashes of Benben to start another life.

It is a continuous cycle of bringing forth and returning to the Source.

Bennu, as such, is a symbol of resurrection, and there were formulae instructing the deceased on how to become the Bennu.

Osiris represents the divine in a mortal form that lives, dies, and is reborn again. It is therefore that the soul of Osiris dwells in the bird Bennu—who is always found near scenes of resurrection.

Every deceased person is Osiris, that will be resurrected and reborn again.

For Bennu will lead all as the resurrected Osiris—being Horus and his disciples – to the Source.

————

Bulls

Three forms of bulls were popular in Ancient Egypt:

– Hap/Hape (Apis),

– Mer-ur (Mnevis, Mnewwer)
– Bakh (Bacis, Buchis).

Variations in "names" are actually words that determine the various function/role of bulls and not regional or historical identification names.

There are also some 'foreign' corruptions in the pronunciation of such "terms" by Western academia.

The specific attribute will be determined in the context. The main various attributes associated with the bull are:

1. Fertility and Sexual Powers

The wild bull, which is a nearly universal symbol for sexual power, symbolizes boundless strength and fertility. Bulls are esteemed for their sexuality; for a single animal can impregnate an entire herd. As such, the wild bull is a symbol for untamed sexual energy.

The universe cannot exist without the ability to replicate (i.e., reproduce). On the metaphysical level, the bull represents this powerful sexual energy that must be tamed and managed.

Clement of Alexandria wrote, in his *Stromata Book V*, chapter VII:

> **"The bull [for the Egyptians] clearly is of the earth itself, and husbandry and food"**

The bulls were/are also associated with fertility rites, as explained by Diodorus, *Book I*, [21, 8-22]:

> **"The consecration to Osiris, however, of the sacred**

bulls, which are given the name of Apis and Mnevis, and the worship of them as gods were observed generally among all the Egyptians, since these animals had, more than any others, rendered aid to those who discovered the fruit of the grain, in connection with both the sowing of the seed and with every agricultural labor from which mankind profits.

2. *Symbolize wild aspects to be tamed*

The bull represents this powerful sexual energy that must be tamed and managed.

Hunting wild animals represents the ability of us humans to control the wild aspects of nature, being within our beings or outside it.

The divine man is depicted dispersing and hunting all kinds of wild animals, including the wild bull.

Controlling the wild in the wild bull can also be achieved through lassoing and taming—as depicted in the Abydos Temple.

3. *Symbolize Strength, determination, hard work*

As noted by Horapollo, to the Egyptians, the bull's horn depicts work. This is similar to the saying in English-speaking countries: *"Take the bull by the Horn"*, a figure of speech that means to take control and get the work done.

4. *Symbolize sacrifice—takes a life to save a life—renewal*

Osiris represents the process, growth, and underlying

cyclical aspects of the universe—the principle that makes life come from apparent death.

The Egyptian word for a young bull is 'Aa G L', simply meaning: *a (male) cycle*.

Osiris represents the rejuvenation/renewal principle in the universe. Therefore, in the Ancient Egypt context, the bull had to suffer a sacrificial death to ensure the life of the community. The sacrifice of the holy animal and the eating of his flesh brought about a state of grace.

Small tablets in Ancient Egyptian tombs sometimes represent a black bull bearing the corpse of a man to its final abode in the regions of the dead. The name of this bull is shown to be Apis, because Osiris represents the state of death in everyone/thing—the divine in mortal form.

Throughout Egypt (and in all eras), bulls are depicted in tombs and temples, to be sacrificed during festivals in order to renew and to rejuvenate life.

It continues to be a common practice in present-day Egypt that young bulls are sacrificed upon the death of a person. The same practice continues in thousands of annual folk saints' festivals in Egypt.

5. Astronomy—Two main representations:

> 1. The bull is one of the zodiac sign, since Ancient Egypt's remotest history.

> 2. As a constellation the *foreleg of the bull* represents the constellation of Ursa major -The big dipper.

—————

Cat

In the *Litany of Re*, Re is described as **The One of the Cat** and **The Great Cat**. The nine realms of the universe are manifested in the cat; for both the cat and the Grand Ennead (meaning nine times—unity) have the same Ancient Egyptian term, 'b.st'. This relationship has found its way to Western culture, where one says that the cat has nine lives (realms).

The cat represents the total harmony within—the sense of internal happiness, contentment, and peace. No wonder that the Ancient Egyptians used the guts of cats to make musical strings for their musical instruments.

Also see Bast as an aspect of the female principle Isis, in a later chapter.

—————

Cows

The cow is the ideal representation for nourishment of all kinds, both physically and metaphysically.

We will highlight, here, a few cow forms.

First is the Celestial cow Mehet-Uret, with her body spangled with stars.

Mehet-Uret (Mehurt, Methyer) represents the primeval water; i.e. the watery abyss of heaven.

Mehet-Uret is associated with Isis in the form of Hathor, representing both physical and metaphysical nourishment.

Water is the source of life and sustenance.

Sometimes the king, as a symbol for Horus, is shown taking milk from her udder.

The Ancient Egyptian texts describe Isis of the 10,000 names, in her nourishment role, as cow-headed:

> *The Cow Heru-sekha, who brings forth all things.*
> *Who nourished the child Horus with her milk.*

The Celestial Cow is also depicted as *seven* cows. Hathor is associated with the number seven, and was referred to as **The Seven Hathors**.

Hesat is a form of Hathor, whose function it is to feed the youngsters.

Hesat represents the metaphysical nourishment (love, caring, singing, etc.) necessary for the growth and well being of the children.

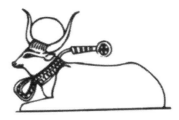

Hathor, as the symbol of spiritual nourishment, also plays an important role in the transformational (funerary) texts, furnishing the spiritual nourishment required by the soul of the deceased.

Crocodile

Various attributes are all related to the crocodile. The specific attribute will be determined in the context as being either 'good' or 'evil'.

1. The crocodile is an aspect manifestation of the solar principle. Reference is made here to Plutarch's *Moralia Volume V*:

> *"The crocodile, certainly, has acquired honor which is not devoid of a plausible reason, but he is declared to be a living representation of God, since he is the only creature without a tongue; for the Divine Word has no need of a voice"*

2. The Egyptian word for crocodile is *Te- MSaHh*. Its verb form is *MaSaHh*—meaning *to rub/anoint*.

The English word Messiah originated also from the Hebrew and Aramic Mashih, which, in its form as a verb

MeSHeH, means 'to anoint'. This word is of Egyptian origin, where *MeSSeH* [the letters in Egyptian are equivalent to *sh* in Hebrew and Aramaic] signified the ritual of anointing Ancient Egyptian Kings with the fat of crocodiles, as was the tradition with all kings in Ancient Egypt since at least 2700 BCE.

Anointing was a ritual of the coronation of the Egyptian King. Thus, the **Christ/Messiah** means **the anointed one**, who is the king.

3. The concept of the birth of the Messiah without sexual intercourse originated in Ancient Egypt. Isis is said to have conceived her son Horus after her husband Osiris' death.

The cosmic force responsible for her impregnation was *MeSSeH*, the crocodile star, as per Spell 148 of the *Coffin Texts*:

> *"The crocodile star (MeSSeH) strikes ... Isis wakes pregnant with the seed of Osiris—namely Horus".*

4. The crocodile also have other significances/roles, as it is portrayed in zodiac and astronomical scenes:

 – As one of the recognized constellations.
 – Always found in zodiac scenes, standing at the beginning of the zodiac cycle, or in his normal horizontal position as an astronomical constellation.

5. The crocodile represents the end of the earthly voyage (death) that is necessary in order to achieve resurrection and eternal life. Without death, there can be no possibility of a return to the source.

Diodorus of Sicily wrote:

"The crocodile is significant of every kind of baseness"

Clement of Alexandria, in his *Stromata Book V*, chapter VII wrote:

"The crocodile symbolizes impudence".

—————

Dog

The dog embodies the cosmic essence of guidance on all levels.

For more details, see Anubis in a later chapter.

—————

Egg

Earlier we talked about the significance of the (dung) Beetle/Scarab and how it forms and rolls its fertile, egg-shaped dung. This symbolizes the *cosmic egg*.

An egg represents the dwelling container where creation process takes place, from a bird's egg to the egg-shaped universe.

The Universal Bubble is egg-shaped and therefore the universal womb/container/bubble is also called Cosmic Egg.

Egyptian texts refer to Khnum as the one who:

"made the cosmic egg"

Khnum is also referred to as:

"Maker of heaven, and earth, and the Tuat, and water and the mountains",

The Cosmic Egg has several inter-related meanings, being:

- the vehicle of the universal spirit
- the embodiment of power/vital force

More about the 'cosmic egg' under Khnum in the next chapter; as well as under Isis in a later chapter of this book.

———————

Falcon

Various attributes are all related to the falcon. The specific attribute will be determined in the context.

1. Falcon(s) represent the universal solar principle, as per Clement of Alexandria in his *Stromata, Book V*, chapter VII:

"—the falcon symbolizes the sun, for it is fiery and destructive (so the Egyptians attribute pestilential diseases to the sun).."

2. The falcon is/was closely associated with Horus, a manifestation of the solar principle.

In his *Moralia Vol. V*, Plutarch states,

"by a falcon they indicate God"

In Clement of Aexandria's *Stromata, Book V*, chapter VII:

> *"A falcon was the symbol of God"*

3. Falcon(s) represent the equinoctial line, as per Clement of Alexandria in his *Stromata, Book V*, chapter VII:

> *"The falcon signifies the equinoctial line, which is high and parched with heat...."*

4. Falcon(s) represent swiftness, as per Diodorus of Sicily:

> *"The falcon signifies to them everything which happens swiftly, since this animal is practically the swiftest of winged creatures. And the concept portrayed is then transferred, by the appropriate metaphorical transfer, to all swift things and to everything to which swiftness is appropriate, very much as if they had been named".*

Also, see Horus in next chapter of this book.

————

Feather

The tall ostrich plume/feather represents the weightlessness of the truth usually identified with Maat by a feather of truth mounted on her head.

Read more about Maat in a later chapter of this book.

————

Frog

Frogs represents conception and procreation; i.e.: the source of life.

Frogs are symbols of abundance, fertility, and resurrection/rebirth.

Frog amulets were/are popular in Egypt for fertility because of the frog's prolific nature.

Read more about frogs under Nun and under Heket in later chapters of this book.

—————

Goose

The goose symbolizes/expresses the word 'son' in the Egyptian language because of that bird's intense love of its offspring, as confirmed by Horapollo.

It is also the goose that laid the golden egg—the source of creation.

Find additional information under Geb in the next chapter of this book.

—————

Hare

The hare's eyes always remain open. Such physical features symbolize the cosmic metaphysical concept for the ever-open, watchful divine eyes.

The long ears of this animal also signify divine hearing/listening.

—————

Heron [Stork/Phoenix]

See Bennu above.

—————

Hippopotamus

Various attributes are all related to the hippopotamus. The specific attribute will be determined in the context of being either 'good' or 'evil'.

1. Being of destructive nature, it is considered One of Seth's animals. This is confirmed in Plurarch's *Moralia, Volume V*:

> *"by the hippopotamus shamelessness"*

2. The huge size of the hippopotamus projects its maternal/child-bearing attributes and is a symbol of fertility.

3. The mother animals are known for fearless protection of their young.

4. As "mother of all", its upright form is found at the beginning of each cycle—such as the zodiac cycle—as depicted in numerous places prior to the Greek era.

5. As the bearer/container of all creation, it is found in all rebirth scenes, cosmic and otherwise.

6. In astronomy, the Hippopotamus is one of the northern circumpolar constellations.

Also see Taurt in a later chapter of this book.

————

Horse

Various attributes are all related to the horse. The specific attribute will be determined in the context.

1. The horse symbolizes fortitude and confidence, as per Clement *Stromata Book V*, chapter VII:

> *"The horse symbolizes fortitude and confidence"*

2. Horse is the hieroglyphic symbol for Noble.

The horse represents the driving force that, when directed correctly, will lead to nobility.

3. Exceptional people are KNIGHTED by the monarch.

This Egyptian concept of nobility is found in present traditions when, because of a person's extraordinary accomplishments, this person is KNIGHTED by no other person but the Monarch.

It is not a coincidence that the English word 'horse' is basically the same as the Egyptian deity Horus.

Horus means *who he is ABOVE.*

4. The horse is also a very beautiful and graceful animal.

The Egyptian word MaHR means both a pony and a dowry—for a maiden is *noble.*

5. Depicted defeating forces of chaos..

The divine man is depicted on Egyptian temples as charging and defeating chaotic forces, represented as foreigners and wild animals.

These depictions are symbolic representations of the inner battle within between the forces of Good and evil.

In mundane sense, Mounted Police everywhere use horses to guide and control crowds. Horse power is also used by police to dissipate disorderly crowds.

We use the term 'Horse power' as a measure of energy.

6. In Egyptian traditions **the human tongue is equated to a horse**. The tongue is the strongest muscle in the human body. The driving force of the horse or tongue controls your destiny.

The symbolism of the horse as the driving force is very powerful indeed.

7. Human and horses are so close that long ago, Ancient Egyptians used horse hair for both the strings and bows of their violin family of instruments. The sound of this instrument is as close as it gets to the human voice.

———

Ibis

Various attributes are all related to the ibis. The specific attribute will be determined by its context.

1. The ibis represents the universal lunar principle, as per Clement' *Stromata Book V*, chapter VII:

"... the ibis, of the moon, likening the shady parts to that which is dark in plumage, and the luminous to the light.

2. The ibis signifies the ecliptic, as per Clement' *Stromata Book V*, chapter VII:

"... the ibis signifies the ecliptic. For the ibis seems, above other animals, to have furnished to the Egyptians the first rudiments of the invention of number and measure, as the oblique line did of circles."

3. The ibis is closely associated with Thoth (Tehuti, Hermes, Mercury), also being of the lunar principle.

4. The Ibis is associated with the Equilateral triangle as per Plutarch in his *Moralia, Vol. V,* about Ancient Egypt, when he wrote:

"By the spreading of Ibis' feet, in their relation to each other and to her bill, she makes an equilateral triangle."

Also see Thoth in the next chapter of this book.

———————

Lions

Various attributes are all related to the lions. The specific attribute will be determined by the context.

1. The lion symbolizes strength, majesty, power, dominion, etc. Clement of Alexandria in his *Stromata Book V*, chapter VII wrote:

..."The lion is for the Egyptians the symbol of strength and prowess"

2. The lioness represents 'The Den Mother' with all that implies—passionate protective tender loving care ... and support and encouragement.

The lioness is represented in Ancient Egypt as **Sekh-Mut**. Sekhmet or Sekhmut is actually two words: Sekh and Mut—meaning Elder or the Den Mother.

3. The lioness represents the fiery aspect of the creative power.

In the *Litany of Re*, Re is described (in one of his 75 forms/attributes) as **The One of the Cat**, and as **The Great Cat**.

4. The lioness is the most fearless animal on earth. In our modern society, the guts and spine are symbols of physical courage. This concept has Ancient Egyptian roots. In the *Papyrus of Ani* [pl. 32 item 42], we read:

"my belly and my spine are Sekh-Mut"

—————

Twin-Lions [Aker]

The main theme of the Ancient Egyptian texts is the cyclical nature of creation being born, living, dying, and regenerating again.

Aker (twin lions) represents the voyage from life to death, east to west, yesterday to tomorrow.

Aker is depicted in pure lion form, or as man-headed lions [sphinx].

They are called the horizon lions.

The lions are always designated as "yesterday" and "tomorrow".

The Egyptian word for a lion is 'Sab-aa', which is the same word for the number 7. One of Osiris' titles was the *Two/Twin Lions*.

In Chapter 17 of *The Book of the Coming Forth By Light*, the deceased, identified with Osiris, says:

I am yesterday, I know the morrow

The significance and function of the number 7 is intimately related to Osiris. Seven is the number of process, growth, and the underlying cyclical aspects of the universe.

A very similar theme to the twin lion Aker is found in the tomb of Queen Nefertari, where we find the rejuvenated green solar deity in a mummiform body.

On the right, by Isis, we read:

> *This is Re who comes to rest in Osiris.*

On the left by Nephthys , we read:

> *This is Osiris who comes to rest in Re.*

Egyptian texts refer to Re and Osiris as the *Twin Souls*.

Etymologically, the relationship between Re and Osiris becomes self-evident.

The Egyptian word for Osiris is *Aus-Ra*.

The word *Aus* means the *power of*, or the *root of*. As such, the name *Ausar* consists of two parts: Aus-Ra, meaning the power of Ra, meaning the re-birth of Ra.

The principle that makes life come from apparent death was/is called Ausar, who symbolizes the power of renewal.

Ausar represents the process, growth, and the underlying cyclical aspects of the universe.

And the back-to-back lions signify this underlying cycle. [The lions from the Hatshepsut Temple]

—————

Rams

Various attributes are all related to the rams. The specific attribute will be determined in the context.

In wall depictions and statues, there are two distinct rams:

> 1. Looped horns that refer to manifestation aspects of creation such as the zodiac Aries Age, that began about 2300 BCE.
> 2. Horizontal horns that refer to conceptual aspects of creation—Khnum.

Our focus here will be on the ram with long, horizontal horns.

The ram in Ancient Egypt was called, Ba.

Ba has several inter-related meanings, being:

> – the vehicle of the universal spirit
> – the embodiment of power/vital force
> – the external manifestation of power

All of the above represents Khnum as an aspect of the creative force of Re (Ra).

Khnum represents the divine process aspect of shaping and forming the universe, both physically and metaphysically.

There are 75 forms or aspects of Re, and Khnum is one of

these aspects. Khnum represents the embodiment of the creative force of Re.

The animal in which Khnum became incarnate was the ram, with flat horns projecting at right angles to his head.

Khnum is depicted in some contexts as a ram-headed bird. This bird represents the Ba of Re—The All encompassing Ba—The Divine Soul.

Also see Khnum, in next chapter of this book.

— — — — —

Scarab

See beetle, above.

— — — — —

Serpents

Various attributes are all related to the serpents. The specific attribute will be determined in the context being either 'good' or 'evil'.

Various depictions are used to correspond to variation of purpose and action—repose, erect, coiled, etc. Various types represent various natures.

Serpents represent various aspects such as:

1. To Symbolize the dual nature of creation—Divine duality within the Unity, Good and evil, etc.

The serpent represents the dualizing principle; the ability of One to divide into Two.

Looking at a serpent, it represents Unity with its undifferentiated length.

It is the Unity that contains the power that results in duality.

In the pre-creation, the female aspect of pre-creation is represented as serpents with their tails being held, representing the potential creation powers within.

The serpent, which is a remarkable individualistic animal, bears both a forked tongue (verbal duality) and a double penis (sexual duality).

The serpent, being the most flexible animal, represents the *provider of all the various forms of creation.*

Neheb Kau—meaning the **provider of forms/attributes**/qualities—was the name given to the serpent representing the primordial serpent/spiral in Ancient Egypt. Neheb Kau is depicted as a two-headed serpent, indicative of the dual spiral nature of the universe.

2. To symbolize divine intellect

As a symbol of duality, the serpent represents intellect; the faculty by which man can break down the whole into its constituent parts. This is analogous to creation, in the sense that multiplicity is created out of unity.

3. Symbol of potency of creation

The ability to multiply is a female aspect. In Nun, the pre-creation state of matter, the female aspect of creation, is represented by snakes.

The female choice of a serpent is also significant. The serpent, as a metaphor for the spiral, is the hieroglyphic symbol used to represent a netert (goddess).

The female aspect, the netert, represents the active potent power in the universe.

4. The Power of Opposition ["Evil"]

In the creation cycle, the dualizing nature of the serpent is the primary cause and effect of multiplication; but the cycle dictates that the multiplicity will be reunited in a new unity again. To achieve reunification, the dualizing nature symbolized by the serpent must be resisted.

Mehen is a coiled serpent, representing one of the forces of light, assisting towards resurrection.

Apep/Apep (Apopis) is a coiled serpent—a form of Seth – representing the power of opposition to resurrection. To overcome such an opposition, combined divine forces are united to defeat Apep (Apopis).

— — — — —

Stork

The stork is known for its migrating and homing instinct. The stork is known worldwide as the bird that carries newborn babies to their new families.

The stork returns to its own nest with consistent precision; hence a migratory bird, par excellence, is the bird chosen for the soul. Ba is usually translated as 'soul'.

The Ba is one of the metaphysical components of the human (and other) beings.

The Ba is immortal. When the Ba departs, the body dies. The Ba is represented as a human-headed bird, which is the opposite of the normal depiction of neteru (gods, goddesses) as human bodies with animal heads (in other words, as the divine aspect of the terrestrial). The Ba may be shown as a stork, or as a falcon. (Also see Bennu, above.)

—————

Vulture

Various attributes are all related to the vultures. The specific attribute will be determined by its context.

1. The vulture represents the barrenness.

2. The vulture express the concept of the 'Virgin Mother' because the female vulture gets impregnated by exposing herself to the sperms carried by winds, and not through direct contact with males. The vulture is therefore a symbol of **virgin birth**—in other words, **purity**.

The most prominent example is that of The Virgin

Mother Isis and her Child Horus—Madonna and the child.

3. The vulture represents Mut, the assimilative power, with all that implies.

4. The vulture is supposed to be particularly zealous in caring for its young.

This symbolic expression of deep spiritual understanding was presented, in the case of vulture, in two main forms and as a bird forming a headdress that appears as a part of the female's head. This form of depiction conveys the particular cosmic function of vultures in the human being.

The other form of vulture depiction is in a purely animal form. This form of depiction conveys the particular cosmic function/attribute, in its purest form.

Vultures are depicted in many locations in Egyptian monuments; in particular, on the ceilings.

Women are depicted wearing a vulture headdress, indicating their spiritual purity.

The most prominent example is that of The Virgin Mother Isis and her Child Horus—Madonna and the child.

More about this subject under Isis, in a later chapter of this book.

—————

Winged Sun

The winged sun represents the success of the individual in overcoming all the obstacles along the spiritual path towards enlightenment, and the ultimate re-unification with the source.

The victorious soul—in the form of winged sun-is always depicted at the gateways of Egyptian temples.

The gateway is the threshold that can only be crossed by the victorious who concurred themselves to achieve reunification with the Source.

More about this subject under Horus, in the next chapter of this book.

CHAPTER 10 : MOST COMMON MALE & ANDROGYNOUS HUMAN FORMS DIVINITIES

In a previous chapter, we explained the choice of a human body as symbol of the universe and how the Egyptian differentiated between earthly and universal human images. In order for creation to exist and to be maintained, this divine energy must be thought of in terms of male and female principles. Therefore, Ancient Egyptians expressed the cosmic energy forces in the terms of netert (female principle) and neter (male principle).

We also discussed earlier animal symbolism. The animal-headed human images represent the divine forces which the Egyptian called Neteru. They are the manifestation of the divine energy in the universe.

In this chapter, we will show the most common male and androgynous forms for the Egyptian divinities/neteru. We have arranged it here in alphabetical order, using the most recognized names for such deities for English-speaking peoples, followed by other [grammatical] forms of each deity. Each deity will be explained with a very brief review of each's metaphysical functions/attributes to help stay away from silly descriptions and focus on the

REAL subtle/deep meanings. It is always helpful to think of 'figures of speech' related to each image to recognize each's nature/behavior/characteristics/attributes.

It is worth repeating that the primary function of these Egyptian Ideograms is to represent thoughts. This means that one must be searching for both the Figurative (an object that stands for one of its qualities) and the Allegorical (an object linked through enigmatic conceptual processes).

We must always keep in mind the relationship between visual forms and their meaning. A visual form may be mimetic or imitative, directly copying features of the object it represents; it may be associative, suggesting attributes which are not visually present such as abstract properties incapable of literal depiction; and finally, it may be symbolic, meaningful only when decoded according to conventions or systems of knowledge which, though not inherently visual, are communicated throughout.

>>> **It should be noted that the digital edition of this book as published in PDF and E-book formats has a substantial number of photographs that compliment the text materials throughout this chapter.**

———

10.1 AMON (AMEN, AMUN)

Amen/Amon/Amun (which means hidden) represents the hidden or occult force underlying creation. Amen represents the spirit that animates the universe and all its components and creatures, even though Amen (The Hidden One) is indefinable himself.

His name has been repeated by many millions of times, for thousands of years, in Ancient Egypt and throughout the rest of the world. His name is still being repeated, nowadays, by people of all faiths, who don't even realize it.

The followers of Judaism, Christianity and Islam all end their prayers by saying "Amen".

In the Egyptian papyrus known as the *Leiden Papyrus J350*, Stanza 600 describes Amen/Amon/Amun as follows:

> *Whose heart is Sia (Knowledge),*
> *Whose Word is Hu (The Word),*
>
> *Whose ka is everything that exists.*
> *Whose ba is Shu, the air, whose heart is Tefnut, the fire,*
>
> *Who is Horus of the double horizon who is in the sky.*
> *Who is the day, who is the night.*
>
> *Who is everybody's guide in all directions.*
> *Who gives birth to everything that is and causes all that exists to live.*

Creation is the sorting out by giving definition, bringing order to all the chaos, both the undifferentiated energy matter and the consciousness of the primeval state. All of the ancient Egyptian accounts of creation exhibit this with well-defined, clearly-identifiable stages.

This hidden force—Amen—is only represented when it animates other aspects/forms of the universe.

Amen is associated with several other deities. When Amen is combined with Re [Ra], as Amen-Re, the joined force represents the animated power of creation.

Amen is the hidden name of Re [Ra].

When Amen combines with Min, as Min-Amen, he symbolizes the creative urge manifested as universal sexuality. [Also see Menu (Min, Amsi, Kamutef), below, in this chapter.]

Amen represents the animation of creation.

————

10.2 ANUBIS (ANBU, UBUAT, WEB-WAWET)

Anubis represents the divine principle of the right sense of direction.

The dog embodies the essence of spiritual guidance. Anubis is often shown as the dog/jackal, or as a human figure with the head of a dog/jackal. The dog/jackal is famous for its reliable homing instinct, day or night. The dog is very useful in searches, and is the animal of choice to guide the blind. As such, it is an excellent choice for guiding the soul of the deceased through the regions of the Duat.

This symbolic expression of deep spiritual understanding was presented in two main forms for Anubis: animal-headed human,s or a pure animal form, as we see here.

When a total animal is presented in Ancient Egypt, it represents a particular function/attribute in its purest form.

When an animal-headed figure is presented, it conveys that particular function/attribute in the human being.

Various associated attributes are all related to the dog. There are several forms of dogs/jackal, shown in various positions in various contexts. The specific attribute will be determined by the context.

We will overview Anubis' functions as:

- The Path Finder
- The alchemist diet
- The Truth Finder

– In our return to our divine origin, we each need a guide/guiding angel that we can trust to lead us on the right direction. This Path Finder is Anubis who represents the right sense of direction—the Divine Guide. The Path Finder is embodied in Anubis as a DoG. DoG is the reverse for GoD—from the world of matter to the world of spirit. The dog/jackal is famous for its reliable homing instinct, day or night. As such, it is an excellent choice for guiding the soul of the deceased through the regions of the Duat.

– The metaphysical role of Anubis, the dog, is reflected in his diet. The dog/jackal feasts on carrion, turning it into beneficial nourishment. In other words, Anubis represents the capacity to turn waste into useful food for the body (and soul) as in the alchemical way of transforming lead into gold.

– The absolute sense of loyalty is embodied into the dog, who is depicted leading the soul of the deceased in the Hall of Judgment where he also ensures accuracy in the symbolic the process of weighing the heart. Anubis represents the right sense of direction in whatever we do, absolute loyalty, and the capacity to turn lead (carrion) into gold (worthiness).

– Anubis also represents the Truth Finder. In the Isis/ Osiris Allegory, it is Anubis that helps Isis find the scattered pieces of Osiris, as *the Manifestor of the Truth.*

To find the broken pieces so as to bind them together is the essence of Religion. The origin of the word Re-ligio-n is the "Latin" *Religio*, which means *to bind together.*

––––––

10.3 ANUBIS AS THE DOG STAR

We will overview Anubis' functions as:

    a. The star of Isis—The Great Provider
    b. The Point of Origin in The Egyptian Calendar

a. Anubis as the Dog Star is always shown leading the arks in their voyages toward the Divine. As such, Anubis represents the Divine Guide.

Sirius, the Dog Star, is the dwelling place of the universal mother Isis.

During the very remote periods of the Ancient Egyptian history, Isis was associated with the star Sabt (Sirius), the brightest star in heaven, which was called, like her, the Great Provider; and whose annual rising ushered in the Nile's inundation.

b. Egypt's ingenious and very accurate calendar was based on the observation and study of Sirius' movements in the sky. This fact is clearly acknowledged in Webster's dictionary, which defines the Sothic (Sabt in Egyptian) year as:

- of having to do with Sirius, the Dog Star.
- Designating or of an Ancient Egyptian cycle or period of time based on a fixed year.

The Ancient Egyptians knew that the full year was slightly over 365¼ days. The earth takes 365.25636 days to complete one revolution around the sun—and that was/is the length of the Egyptian Sothic Year. [More details can be found in *Ancient Egyptian Culture Revealed* by Moustafa Gadalla.]

Let the Anubis attributes within you guide you in the right direction.

— — — — —

10.4 APIS [EPAPHUS, HAPIS]

It takes a life to save a life. Osiris came to Earth for the benefit of mankind, and was sacrificed and became the Lord of Judgment in the other world. Osiris is the allegorical renewal of life. One must die—figuratively—to be born again.

We find a similar and later conception in the Abraham religions; that Abraham sacrificed a ram to save the life of his son.

One of the most important rituals in the Egyptian annual festivals, since ancient times, is the ritual sacrifice of the bull, which represents the renewal of cosmic forces through the death and resurrection of the bull deity.

The Egyptians connected Apis, both living and dead, with Osiris. He was the son of Osiris, as well as of Ptah, and was the "living image of Osiris". After the death of his body, his soul was thought to go to heaven, where it joined itself to Osiris and formed with him the dual-god Asar-Hepi, or Osiris-Apis. Bull is basically the incarnation of Osiris. Classical writers of antiquities assert that Apis the bull was sacrificed for Osiris since the time of Mena, 5,000 years ago.

In the Ancient Egyptian traditions, wine was sacrificed for the blood of Osiris.

Egyptians felt obligated to eat the meat of the sacrificial bull and to drink wine during festivities in order to receive the divine blessing.

That the wine was sacrificed for the blood of Osiris is depicted in practically all Egyptian tombs.

The walls of the Ancient Egyptian tombs show vintners pressing new wine, and wine-making is everywhere as a constant metaphor of spiritual processes and the themes of transformation and inner power.

The wine-making process of growing, harvesting, pressing and fermenting is a metaphor for spiritual processes.

The soul, or the portion of god within, causes the divine ferment in the body of life. It's developed there (as on the vine) by the sun of man's spiritual self. The fermented potency of wine was, at its deepest spiritual level, a symbol of the presence of the incarnated god within the spiritually aware person.

In the *Book of the Dead*, Osiris is addressed as the "**Bull of Amentet**"; i.e., "**Bull of the Other world**".

In Ancient Egypt, the Mother deity, Isis, had a son who, in the form of a bull, was sacrificed annually in order to assure the cycle of the seasons and the continuity of Nature.

As per present practices, ancient writers asserted that it was the mother who was chosen to produce a calf with particular qualities (he was The Bull of His Mother—so to speak). Herodotus, in describing him, says:

> *"Apis, also called Epaphus, is a young bull, whose mother can have no other offspring, and who is reported by the Egyptians to conceive from lightning*

sent from heaven, and thus to produce the bull-god Apis."

Religious connotations of this sacrifice are an echo of a sacrifice in the sacrament, where we are reminded of Christ's death so that mankind might be saved. In essence, this is a genuine religious drama in which, as in the Catholic Mass, a god is worshiped and sacrificed.

In practically all Egyptian tombs of all eras, we find the selection of the young calf and its separation from his mother near the "false door", under the observation of the tomb occupant.

Diodorus, in *Book I*, [85, 3-5], explains the rejuvenation powers of the sacrificial bull:

> *"Some explain the origin of the honor accorded this bull in this way, saying that at the death of Osiris his soul passed into this animal, and therefore up to this day he always passed into its successors at the times of the manifestation of Osiris".*

Osiris represents the process, growth, and the underlying cyclical aspects of the universe—the principle that makes life come from apparent death.

Osiris represents the rejuvenation/renewal principle in the universe. Therefore, in the Ancient Egypt context, the bull had to suffer a sacrificial death to ensure the life of the community. The sacrifice of the holy animal, and the eating of his flesh, brought about a state of grace.

Small tablets in Ancient Egyptian tombs sometimes represent a black bull bearing the corpse of a man to its final abode in the regions of the dead. The name of this bull is shown to be Apis, because Osiris represents the state of death in everyone/thing—the divine in mortal form.

Throughout Egypt (and in all eras), bulls are depicted in tombs and temples, to be sacrificed during the festivals to renew and to rejuvenate life.

[For additional information, also see Bulls in a prior chapter of this book.]

—————

10.5 ATON [ADON]

Aton is the disk of the sun, one of the physical manifestations of Re (Ra).

Aton is one of a multitude of divinities, but it was not a new idea that was introduced by Akhenaton (1367-1361 BCE). Aton is found in Egyptian texts that go back at least to the 12th Dynasty (1991-1783 BCE).

It has been said (and repeated) that Akhenaton exalted Aton over and above the other aspects/powers/neteru of the One Supreme God.

As mentioned in chapter 4 of this book, Adon/Aton is a title meaning *Lord*. Adonai in Hebrew means *my Lord*. The last two letters, 'ai', of the word is a Hebrew pronoun meaning 'my' or 'mine' and signifying possession. 'Adon,' meaning Lord, was correctly noted by Sigmund Freud as the Hebrew word for the Egyptian Aton/Aten. As the Egyptian 't' becomes 'd' in the Hebrew tongue, Adon is the

Hebrew equivalent of the Egyptian Aton. Thus, Adon and Aton/Aten are one and the same.

[Read more about Akhenaton in either Ancient Egyptian Roots of Christianity and/or Historical Deception: The Untold Story of Ancient Egypt – 2nd ed., both by Moustafa Gadalla.]

————

10.6 ATUM [ATEM, ATOM, ATAM]

Earlier we explained what Atum/Atem/Atom/Atam represents [see chapter 2].

————

10.7 BES

Bes represents the unknown extraordinary powers.

Bes is depicted as a grotesque dwarf with a mask-like face. The dwarf's small size disguises his/her tremendous strength.

Dwarfs demonstrate remarkable control over the spiritual and physical environment. They are instruments both for reward and punishment.

Bes, the powerful dwarf, is found in Egypt (since at least 5,000 years ago) in the form of statues, amulets, and different artwork as well as depictions in temples and tombs throughout Egypt.

This is a statue found in Saqqara from Old Kingdom. It was discovered by the French Egyptologist, Auguste Mariette, in the 19th century.

Dwarfs are depicted in Ancient Egyptian tombs, 4,500 years ago, performing metal working—a common application of their extraordinary physical and metaphysical powers.

Bes, the dwarf, is also associated with childbirth, joy, music, and as being a protector against snakebites and a helper of women during childbirth.

Bes is found in papyri of all ages associated with rebirth, a common Egyptian theme, is depicted underneath the bed, and as such is found in amulets; often in ithyphallic form.

From the time of Amenhotep III more than 3,400 years ago, we find Bes, the dwarf, depicted in his usual place underneath the couch in the Birth Chamber of the Luxor Temple.

The details of the scene are found in ALL Egyptological references despite the fact that the wall depiction is so hard to photograph and must be seen on location.

A very similar scene from the Luxor Temple is found in the Dendera Temple.

Bes the dwarf is found in Birth houses everywhere, as shown here in a column capital in the Edfu Temple Complex, where he is protecting Madonna and her child.

— — — — —

10.8 GEB (SEB, KEB)

Geb (Seb, Keb) represents the material/physical aspects of the universe.

Geb is depicted as a man bearing a goose upon his head.

This representation is the source of the worldwide notion about *the goose that laid the egg* from which the world was hatched.

Geb is the consort of Nut. More information about this combined significance is found under Nut in the next chapter of this book.

Geb is often depicted reclining under Nut, fallen to earth and raised on one arm with one knee bent [shown in depictions under Shu, later this chapter].

—————

10.9 HAPI [HEPR]

Hapi [Hepr] is depicted in the form of a man that has a big belly and a single female breast, representing plenti-fulness His breasts are androgynous, indicating fertility. He wears upon his head a clump of flowers in both open and closed positions.

Hapi [Hepr] is represented in Egypt under two forms—singularly, or in twin mirror image form in the symbolic rites related to the ceremony of *Uniting the Two Lands*. [This has nothing to do with the geography of Egypt. See *Egyptian Cosmology* by Moustafa Gadalla, for explanations.]

Ancient Egyptian texts do not relate him to the River Nile, as incorrectly published by Western academia. As Egyptologist Budge correctly noticed, Hapi was identified with all the neteru (gods, goddesses) and, in turn, it follows as a matter of course that the attributes of each of them were ascribed to him, as per *Book Of Dead* 190-1.

There is a scene in Medinet Habu Temple in Luxor that shows a sitting Hapi. Behind him is Bennu on Benben, an indication of a very early role in the creation process. He is related to Nun—the original state of pre-creation, and in such cases he is depicted in a blue color. He may be equated to '*Old Man River*' as the source of things and provider of life in the form of water. In this regard, he is depicted everywhere in Egyptian monuments as the '*model offerer*' providing the offers to the neteru (gods, goddesses).

––––––

10.10 HERISHEF (HARSAPHIS, ARSHAPHES, ARSAPHES)

Herishef (Harsaphis) represents the perpetual cycle of existence—the cycle of life and death—as symbolized by Re and Osiris.

Re is the living neter (god) who descends into death to become Osiris, the neter of the dead. Osiris ascends and comes to life again as Re. The creation is continuous; it is a flow of life progressing towards death. But out of death, a new Re is to be born, sprouting new life.

Re is the cosmic principle of energy that moves toward death, and Osiris represents the process of rebirth. Thus, the terms of life and death become interchangeable: life means slow dying, and death means resurrection to new life. The dead person in death is identified with Osiris, but he will come to life again and will be identified with Re.

The perpetual cycle of Osiris and Re dominates the Ancient Egyptian texts. A vivid example can be found in the tomb of Queen Nefertari (wife of Ramses II), where there is a well-known representation of Herishef (Harsaphis) as a mummiform body with the head of a ram, accompanied by Isis on the right and Nephthys on the left. The inscription, right and left, reads:

"This is Re who comes to rest in Osiris.
This is Osiris who comes to rest in Re."

[Also see Khnum, Re and Osiris in this chapter.]

––––––

10.11 HORUS [HERU]

Heru means *He who is above*. As such, Horus (Heru) represents the realized divine principle.

Heru (Horus) results from the heavenly marriage between Isis and the holy ghost of Osiris.

As the model of earthly existence, Horus is represented in

several forms and aspects corresponding with the stages in the process of spiritualization, and is not just limited to being a falcon-headed deity.

We will be covering Horus' roles in the following areas:

1. Horus in the Sequence of creation
2. Horus as symbol of the Heart
3. Horus as The Fifth Star
4. Horus sand Osiris—Like Father Like Son
5. Horus and Isis—Child and Madonna
6. Horus Disciples (Sons)
7. Horus and Seth—The Inner Struggle
8. Horus—as the initiate deity—The five Phases of Horus
9. House of Horus—Het-Hor (as the womb/matrix and shrine)

1. Horus in the Sequence of creation

The ninth Stanza of the Ancient Egyptian *Leiden Papyrus J350* recalls the Grand Ennead, the first nine entities that came forth from Nun.

The first of the Grand Ennead was Atam, who came into being out of Nun, the cosmic ocean. Atam then spat out the twins Shu and Tefnut, who in turn gave birth to Nut and Geb, whose union produced Osiris, Isis, Seth and Nephthys.

The nine aspects of the Grand Ennead emanate from, and are circumscribed about, The Absolute. They are not a sequence, but a unity—interpenetrating, interacting, and interlocked.

They are the generator of all creation, as symbolized by Horus, who, according to the *Leiden Papyrus*, Stanza No. 50, is:

"...the offspring of the nine-times-unity of neteru"

Since the human being is a universal replica, a human child is normally conceived, formed, and born in nine months. Number 9 marks the end of gestation and the end of each series of numbers.

Horus as number 10 is the highest number of the original unity. At ten, Horus is a new One. As such, he represents the return to the Source and thus becomes the initiate deity, as will be discussed further, later herein.

2. Horus—The Symbol of the Heart

In the Ancient Egyptian traditions, the active faculties of Atam—and thus the Great Ennead—were intelligence, which was identified with the heart and represented by Horus, a solar neter (god); and action, which was identified with the tongue and represented by Thoth—a lunar neter (god).

Heru   Tehuti

The solar and lunar neteru stress the universal character. In the *Shabaka Stele* (dated from the 8th century BCE; but a reproduction of a 3rd Dynasty text), we read:

> *"There came into being as the heart (Horus), and there came into being as the tongue (Thoth), the form of Atam".*

One thinks with the heart and acts with the tongue, as described on the *Shabaka Stele*:

> *"The Heart thinks all that it wishes, and the Tongue delivers all that it wishes".*

The significance of heart and tongue permeates Ancient Egyptian texts and was subsequently adopted in "Sufism".

Horus represents conscience and will, and is identified with the heart. Thoth represents deliverance and manifestation, and is identified with the tongue.

The combined action of Horus and Thoth governs the actions of all living organisms—large and small. Each action, voluntary or involuntary, is the result of cause and effect. As such, Horus represents the cause and Thoth represents the effect.

The universal rule of cause and effect, symbolized by the functions of the heart and tongue, is found on the Egyptian *Shabaka Stele* (716-701 BCE), as follows:

> *"The Heart and the Tongue have power over all . . . the neteru (gods), all men, all cattle, all creeping things, and all that lives. The Heart thinks all that it wishes, and the Tongue delivers all that it wishes".*

– The most depicted duality in Ancient Egypt is that of Horus and Thoth, solar and lunar deities.

– Horus = heart and Thoth = tongue

– Horus = closed bud/conscience and Thoth = open blossom/manifestation.

3. Horus as The Fifth Star

In Ancient Egypt, the symbol for a star was drawn with five points. The Star was the Egyptian symbol for both destiny and the number five.

Five-pointed stars are the homes of successfully departed souls, as stated in the *Unas Funerary Texts* (known as *Pyramid Texts*), Line 904:

> *"be a soul as a living star "*

Horus is the personification of the goal of all initiated teachings, and therefore is associated with the number five; for he is the fifth, after Isis, Osiris, Seth and Nephthys.

Horus is also the number 5 in the right angle triangle of 3:4:5, as confirmed by Plutarch. In Plutarch's *Moralia, Vol. V,* we read:

> *"Three [Osiris] is the first perfect odd number: four is a square whose side is the even number two [Isis]; but five [Horus] is in some ways like to its father, and in some ways like to its mother, being made up of three and two. And panta (all) is a derivative of pente (five), and they speak of counting as "numbering by fives".*

Five incorporates the principles of polarity (II) and reconciliation (III). All phenomena, without exception, are polar in nature, treble in principle. Therefore, five is the key to understanding the manifested universe, as per Plutarch, on Egyptian thinking:

"And panta (all) is a derivative of pente (five)."

The significance and function of the number five in Ancient Egypt is indicated by the manner in which it was written. The number 5 in Ancient Egypt was written as 2 (II) above 3 (III), or as a five-pointed star. In other words, number 5 is the result of the relationship between number 2 and number 3.

Two symbolizes the power of multiplicity – the female, mutable receptacle – while Three symbolizes the male. This was the 'music of the spheres'; the universal harmonies played out between these two primal male and female universal symbols of Osiris and Isis, whose heavenly marriage produced the child Horus.

Stanzas 50 and 500 of the Ancient Egyptians' *Leiden Papyrus J350* (whose first word *dua* means at the same time *five* and *to worship*) consists of hymns of adoration exalting the marvels of Creation.

4. Horus and Osiris—Like Father Like Son

In the Bible teachings, Christ is sometimes referred to as the "Son of God" and at other times simply as God. In John's Gospel, Christ says: *"I and the Father are one."*

The history of political and doctrinal struggles within the Church during and after the 4th century has largely been written in terms of the disputes over the nature of God and Christ and the relationship between them.

All the "apparent" conflicting theories about these natures can be explained in the Ancient Egyptian context of the relationship between Osiris—the Father—and his Divine Son—namely, Horus. In a way, Osiris and Horus were complimentary; each of the other.

The interchangeable relationship between the Father and the Son is eloquently illustrated here, where Horus is being born out of Osiris after Osiris' death, with the sun disk rising with the newborn. This concept is translated into the common expression, *"The King is dead. Long live the King."* As if to say, *"Osiris is dead. Long live Horus."*

Nebt-Het
(Nephthys)   Heru (Horus), rising
                             from Ausar (Osiris)   Auset
                                                                    (Isis)

The Egyptians believed in the anthropomorphic divinity, or Horus, (Christ) ideal, whose life in this world and the world beyond was typical of the ideal life of man. The chief embodiments of this divinity were Osiris and his son, Horus (Christ). Neither, however, was ever regarded as historical.

Osiris represents the mortal man carrying within himself the capacity and power of spiritual salvation. Every Egyptian's hope was/is resurrection in a transformed body and immortality which could only be realized through the death and resurrection of Osiris within each person. Osiris symbolizes the subconscious—the capacity to act, to do; while Horus symbolizes consciousness: will and the potential to act; to do.

5. Horus and Isis—Child and Madonna

Now that we talked about the father-son relationship, we follow by talking about the relationship between the son and his Virgin Mother Isis.

Isis' role in the Egyptian Model Story and the story of the Virgin Mary are strikingly similar; for both were able to conceive without male impregnation. Horus was conceived and born after the death of Isis' husband and, as such, she was revered as the Virgin Mother.

More information is to be found under Isis in the next chapter of this book and in the book *Ancient Egyptian Roots of Christianity* by Moustafa Gadalla.

6. Horus Disciples (Sons)

Like the Biblical Jesus, Horus was always followed or accompanied by disciples.

The four disciples (commonly and mistakenly translated as "sons") of Heru (Horus) are:

> Duamutef (Tuamutef)—jackal/dog-headed.
> Amset (Imset, Imsety) —human-headed.
> Hapi—baboon-headed.
> Kebsennuf (Qebsennuf)—hawk-headed.

Sometimes they are depicted in all human form, following Horus behind the Bird of origin, Bennu.

In funerary scenes, the four disciples (sons) are depicted as little mummiform figures standing on an opened lotus.

The four disciples (sons) of Horus are in charge of the protection and advancement of the viscera contained in the canopic jars of the deceased. Each disciple was himself under the protection of a netert (goddess), and each was associated with one of the cardinal points, as follows:

Head—	Shape—Head	Netert—of Head	Jar of	Direction
Duamutef—	jackal/dog—	Neith—	stomach—	north
Kebsennuf—	hawk—	Selkis—	intestines—	south
Hapi—	baboon—	Nephthys—	lungs—	east
Amset—	man—	Isis—	liver—	west

More about the metaphysical significance of the body parts contained in the jars are in the next chapter of this book, under the listed netert (goddesses).

7. Horus and Seth—The Inner Struggle

In the Egyptian allegorical model story, there are a series of battles between Horus and Seth. Such illustrates how life is a continuous quest for the divine within ourselves, as symbolized by Horus and Seth.

The archetypal inner struggle in the Egyptian model is symbolized in the struggle between Horus and Seth. It is the archetypal struggle between opposing forces. Horus, in this context, is the divine man, born of nature, who must do battle against Seth, his own kin, representing the power of opposition and not evil in the narrow sense.

Seth represents the concept of opposition in all aspects of life (physically and metaphysically).

We must continuously learn and evolve, like Heru (Horus), whose name means *He Who is Above*. In other words, we must strive to reach higher and higher.

We learn and act by affirmation of the Horus in each of us, and by negating the Seth within us. The obstacles within each of us, represented by Seth, must be controlled and/ or overcome. Such obstacles are the ego, laziness, over-confidence, arrogance, evasiveness, indifference, etc.

In the Egyptian model, Seth represents the wilderness and foreign aspects within each of us. It is therefore that in Ancient Egyptian temples, tombs, and texts, human vices are depicted as foreigners (the sick body is sick because it is/was invaded by foreign germs). Foreigners are depicted as subdued—arms tightened/tied behind their backs—to portray inner self-control.

The most vivid example of self-control is the common depiction of the Pharaoh (The Perfected Man) on the outer walls of Ancient Egyptian temples, subduing/controlling foreign enemies—the enemies (impurities) within.

Horus is victorious.

8. Horus—as the initiate deity

Heru (Horus), in the Ancient Egyptian language, means **He who is above**. As such, Heru (Horus) represents the realized divine principle. Heru (Horus) is the personification of the goal of all initiated teachings, and is always depicted accompanying the realized soul to the Source.

In the Ancient Egyptian allegory, Heru (Horus) brought Ositis to life. On Judgment Day, Horus shows the Way to Osiris. He acts as a mediator between the deceased and Osiris. All Egyptians wanted/want Horus to bring them (dead) to life.

Likewise, in Christianity the Christian motif was/is based on the need for a mediator – a son of god – as an all-powerful shepherd and a begotten savior living among the common man.

The Way of Horus/Christ Horus declares, in *The Egyptian Book of Coming Forth by Light* (incorrectly known as *The Egyptian Book of the Dead*) [c. 78]:

> *"I am Horus in glory";*
> *"I am the Lord of Light";*
> *"I am the victorious one .*
> *. . I am the heir of endless time";*
> *"I am he that knoweth the paths of heaven."*

The Ancient Egyptian verses above were echoed later in Jesus' words, *"I am the light of the world,"* and again, *"I am the way, the truth and the life."*

Our progression is symbolized by Horus. One of his "titles" is **the Lord of the Ladder.**

As the model of earthly existence, Heru (Horus) is represented in several forms and aspects that correspond with the stages in the process of spiritualization.

The five most common forms of Horus are:

1. **Hor-Sa-Auset**, which means Horus, Son of Isis (Horsiesis or Harsiesis).

He is often shown as an infant being suckled by Isis, which is identical to the later Christian representation of the Madonna and her child.

In the lifespan of a person, this is the age of total dependency.

2. **Heru-p-Khart/Hor-Pa-Khred**, which means Heru the Child. **Harpocrates**.

He is often shown with his forefinger on his mouth, symbolizing the taking in of knowledge.

This is the age of learning, with an inquisitive mind.

3. **Horus Behdety or Apollo** is Heru, who avenged the death of his father and flew up to heaven in the form of a winged disk.

This represents the stage in our lives of working and struggling to achieve higher spiritual realms so that one can fly up to heaven, victorious.

Depictions of Horus Behdety are found in most Ancient Egyptian structures, but more prominently at the Edfu Temple.

4. **Heru-ur**, which means Heru (Horus) the Elder or Heru the Great or **Haroeris/Harueris**.

Heru-ur (Haroeris) is usually depicted as a hawk-headed male divinity wearing the double crown. This represents the stage of reaching the age of wisdom; and hence the title, Heru the Elder.

Heru-ur (Horus) The Elder is depicted in numerous

Ancient Egyptian temples, but more prominently at Kom Ombo.

5. **Hor.Akhti/Horachti**, which means Horus on/of the Horizon—a form of a new morning sun. Harmachis is its Greek rendering.

Hor.Akhti signifies the renewal/new beginning; a new day. This will be manifested in the form of **Ra-Hor.Akhti.**

Also see Re-Hor-Akhti below, in this chapter.

9. House of Horus—Het-Hor

Het-hor is commonly translated by western Egyptologists as *"house of Horus"*. The first part—*Het*, translated as "house", has a bigger meaning than a simple house. It actually means the womb as a Matrix within which something originates, takes form, and develops into full maturity.

Horus represents the realized divine principle—and Horus is recognized by various names/attributes as he develops from infancy to maturity within the cosmic womb.

The final destination is unification with the creator as Re. At this point, the realized soul becomes Re-Hor-akhti. It is therefore that Het-hor is called the Lady of the West, residence of Horus—as Re-Hor-achti.

The realized soul reaches the ultimate goal depicted as falcon in green, the color of rejuvenation/renewal.

Hail to the Glorious One.

More about Hathor (Het-hor)in the next chapter of this book.

—————

10.12 KKEPRI (KHEPRA)

[see Beetle in previous chapter and Re in this chapter]

—————

10.13 KKNUM

Khnum represents the divine process aspect of shaping and forming the universe, both physically and metaphysically.

To better illustrate Khnum's divine role, Khnum is usually depicted as a ram-headed deity working at his potter's wheel, fashioning men and all living creatures out of clay. This Egyptian concept is reminiscent of the biblical account of God fashioning Adam from clay.

An important distinction must be made here regarding

the ram depiction in the Ancient Egyptian monuments between two forms of Rams:

1. Rams with Looped horns—as we find in the Karnak Temple and as one of the 12 signs of the zodiac. This ram represents the Aries Age that began about 2300 BCE.

2. Rams with horizontal horns. It is this ram that with horizontal horns that represents Khnum.

Khnum is very ancient, and we find his name preserved by the Gnostics, of early Christianity. Not only that but is also mentioned in the *Old Testament*.

Khnum represents and was always recognized throughout the ancient Egyptian history as a significant aspect of the creation process of the universe.

Khnum's representations and shrines are found in many places throughout Egypt and are not limited to the cataract region in conjunction with the annual flood season of the River Nile in Egypt.

Khnum is usually shown working at his potter's wheel, fashioning men out of clay. Khnum, however, represents the molding of all matters, thoughts, plans, etc. As such,

Khnum is associated with other neteru (gods/goddesses) such as Re, Ptah, etc.

The following main subjects related to Khnum will be discussed:

1. Khnum—the Ram of Re
2. His attributes/names
3. Khnum—The Primordial Shaping Force
4. Khnum—Ruler of Time
5. The Man Maker—the Mini Universe

1. Khnum—the Ram of Re

Re represents this primeval creative force, which causes the transformation of the pre-creation chaotic state to organized and well-structured forms.

The *Litany of Re* describes the demarcated aspects of the creative principle—being recognized as the neteru (gods/goddesses) whose actions and interactions in turn created the universe.

As such, all the Egyptian neteru who took part in the creation process are aspects of Re.

There are 75 forms or aspects of Re—and Khnum is one of these aspects.

Khnum represents the embodiment of the creative force of Re.

The animal in which Khnum became incarnate was the ram, with flat horns projecting at right angles to his head.

The word *Ram* means the embodiment of Ra [Re].

Ram = Ra – m; whereby 'm' is a formative letter.

Ram in Egypt was also called **Ba**.

Ba has several inter-related meanings:

– the vehicle of the universal spirit
– the embodiment of power/vital force
– the external manifestation of power

All of the above represents Khnum as an aspect of the creative force of Ra.

Khnum is depicted in some context as a ram-headed bird. This bird represents the Ba of Ra [Re]—The All encompassing Ba—The Divine Soul.

2. His attributes/names

The word or name or more accurately the *verb*, Khnum is connected with words that mean,

"to build"
"to fashion"
"to put together"—both intellectually and physically

Here we see the intellectual as well as the physical shaping and forming aspects of the Universe, in whole and in part.

- In whole, Khnum represents the fashioning of the Cosmic Egg—The Whole Universe.

- In part, Khnum represents the fashioning of the divine forces; being the neteru as well as mankind and everything else that exists.

In light of the significance of Khnum in the creation of the universe—in whole and in part, the Ancient Egyptian texts referred to Khnum as:

- *The father, in the beginning.*
- *The weaver.*
- *Father of the fathers of the neteru*(gods and goddesses).
- *The modeler.*
- *Supporter of the sky upon; raised up of the same in the firmament.*
- *Lord of things created in himself* (reference to the Cosmic Egg).
- *Governor of the House of Life*—being the Cosmic Egg.
- *Maker of heaven and earth, and the Tuat, and water and the mountains.*
- *The Maker of things that are.*
- *Creator of things that shall be; Source of the lands.*

3. Khnum—The Primordial Shaping Force

Khnum representing the Primordial Shaping Force is found prominently in all creation texts and depictions.

In this well-known depiction of the created universe, Khnum is depicted as being outside the universal bubble—indicative of the intellectual aspect of planning and executing of the orderly and well thought out creation plan. In this regard, Khnum is described in the Egyptian text as, **The Weaver.**

The Egyptians insisted that creation was not an accident, but was a pre-conceived plan.

In the same scene, Khnum is also found within the universal bubble on both sides of Shu, the divine agent of expansion, maintaining the stability of the universe.

This depiction is reinforced by ancient Egyptian text describing Khnum as:

> *"Supporter of the sky upon, raised up of the same in the firmament".*

The firmament here is Nut, with her star-studded body arching over heaven.

Another affirmation that Khnum represents the primordial cosmic shaping force is a wall text in Esna that calls Khnum

> *"the prop of heaven who hath spread out the same with his hands"*

The Universal Bubble is egg-shaped and therefore the universal bubble is also called the Cosmic Egg.

Egyptian texts refer to Khnum as the one who:

> *"made the cosmic egg"*

Khnum is also referred to as:

> *"Maker of heaven, and earth, and the Tuat, and water and the mountains".*

In a larger sense, Khnum represents the Cosmic Egg and all creation within it, as affirmed by references to his attributes in the Egyptian texts as being:

– The modeler.

– Lord of things created in himself. (reference to the Cosmic Egg)

– Governor of the House of Life—being the Cosmic Egg.

– Maker of heaven and earth, and the Tuat, and water and the mountains.

– The Maker of things that are.

– Creator of things that shall be.

As we stated earlier, the Cosmic Egg has same definitions as the ram-headed Khnum. Khnum is therefore almost always depicted next to or within the Cosmic Egg.

4. Khnum—Ruler of Time

The Cosmic Egg, being the universal bubble, is indicative of the living SPACE of the universe. The other side of Space is Time. Time and space are two sides of the same coin, which is perfectly represented in the science of astronomy and its application, astrology. Scientists now agree that there is a very close connection between space and time—so close that you cannot have one without the other.

In Ancient Egypt, the representative of space—being Khnum-is also the representative of time.

Khnum is the Ruler of Space—and TIME.

The cyclical nature of the universe manifests itself into various and inter-related cycles:

– lunar
– solar

– zodiacal

– Sothic—related to the Sirius, the Dog Star

All these cycles are depicted in Esna Temple, where Khnum and his attributes are prominent.

Older Ancient Egyptian texts describe his role as the *Ruler of Time,* as follows:

> *"Khnum who coordinated*
> *the movements of*
> *the sun and the moon*
> *at various seasons,*
> *and built up the year."*

In addition to Esna, we find Khnum depicted with the Firmament deity Nut—with her star studded body—in practically every tomb and temple throughout Ancient Egyptian history.

Nut is always associated with the zodiacal cycle and its 12 zodiacal signs, and has been since more than 5,000 years ago.

The Sothic cycle, which is the basis for the Ancient Egyptian year, is the ONLY accurate calendar in the history of the world.

Khnum was closely associated with the female deity Satis, who is associated with Sirius, the star of Isis that ushered in the beginning of the Ancient Egyptian New Sothic Year.

5. The Man Maker—The Mini Universe

Just as Khnum represents the divine shaping force of the whole universe, Khnum is also depicted fashioning the image or the miniature universe—man—on a potter's wheel.

The well-known Ancient Egyptian illustration showing Khnum, the Divine Potter, at his potter's wheel, fashioning men from clay, was echoed thousands of years later in Isaiah, 64:8:

> *"Yet, O Lord, thou art our Father; we are the clay, and thou art our potter; we are all the work of thy hand".*

Khnum is usually found next to the Egyptian Madonna and her child Horus.

Horus represents life on earth—and his divine Maker Khnum is found next to him.

While The Virgin Mother Isis nurses Horus, Khnum is showing them a copy of Horus.

The Egyptians have always believed that there are 2 Earths or lands—one that we live on and another one that our opposite image lives on. The two were separated at the time of birth and are connected again—upon earthly departure – where they will meet their maker.

———

10.14 KHONSU (KHONS)

Khonsu is depicted in human form (often mummiform) with a child's sidelock of hair, sometimes hawk-headed.

The word Khnosu means *elusive* like a phantom.

Khonsu is a lunar deity and is mostly found with the female solar deity Sekh-mut, the lioness.

Sometimes he is depicted alone and other times with Maat or Mut.

Khonsu represents the cyclical nature of the moon and its associated effects of fertility, conception, childbirth, healing, etc.

The elusive Khnosu is always found behind the scene and its activity.

Khonsu maybe referred to as the 'dark side of the moon'.

———————

10.15 MIN (MENU, AMSI, KAMUTEF)

Min (Menu, Amsi, Kamutef), maybe recognized in some publications as Min-Amen.

Min (Menu) or Amsi represents the divine aspect of fertility, a creative urge manifested as the universal sexuality.

To depict the concept of fertility in a visual form, an erect phallus is the obvious choice.

It is therefore that Menu (Min, or more accurately, Menwi) is depicted with an erect phallus, the flail cocked over his upraised arm.

As such, he is associated with Zeus and his thunderbolt.

But there is deeper meaning to both the name and the depiction format. The name/word Menu/Menwi means (male) *sperm*—which is compatible with the concept of fertility as well as the depiction of an erect phallus.

As for the depiction, not only is an erect phallus the ideal representation of fertility, but also WHERE the Egyptians placed it on a depicted human figure reinforces the concept of fertility.

It should be noted that the erect phallus is depicted near the navel of the human figure to express both the cause of fertility (erect phallus) and the effect—such as the birth – represented by the navel.

Min/Menu/Menwi represents the power of generation, or the reproductive force of nature.

————

10.16 NEFERTUM

Nefertum represents the perpetual renewed creation.

Renewed creation is evident by saying *Nefertum*, which consists of two words:

> – The first part—Nefer basically means—*anew or renewed*.
> – The second part—Tum or Tem – means *complete*.

The Ancient Egyptian texts describe Nefer-Tum as being born anew each morning from the lily.

As far back as 4400 years ago, we read in the commonly-known *Pyramid Texts*, addressing the Pharaoh Unas:

> *"Rise like Nefer-Tum from the lily and to come forth on the horizon every day".*

We should point out here that Nefer-Tum is related to the lily and NOT the Lotus. The depiction and references clearly show the lily.

The lily represents whiteness, as equated to purity.

To represent the perpetual renewal creation, Nefer-Tum is depicted in two related forms:

– as a man with a lily flower headdress,

– rising out of a lily, as shown in the next depiction.

Rising out of a lily is indicative of rebirth.

The lily is rising out of the water after it has been submerged. This is the same exact concept and practice of Baptism. To be born or reborn of the purity of a lily is the embodiment of the principle of conscious creation.

Nefer-Tum represents the ability to mature; to come out.

Nefer-Tum represents the born-again, starting a new/ renewed phase.

Nefer-Tum is referred to in the Egyptian texts as the ***neter of lily***.

With the special aroma of the lily and Nefer-Tum rising, smelling like a rose, Nefer-Tum is considered to be the *patron of perfumes and aromatics.*

The perfume of the lily is its spiritualized essence, representing the true odor of sanctity.

———

Nefer-Tum: The Holy Spirit of The Triad—Ptah Sokaris Nefertum

Nefer Tum, as the agent of renewed creation, is the third of the triad:

Ptah – Sokaris – Nefertum

Nefertum is described in the Ancient Egyptian texts as:

'the successor of Ptah and Sokaris.'

This triad is the Egyptian version of:

Father Son Holy Spirit.

This trinity embodies the concept that *one must die to be born again*.

A new/raised consciousness is equivalent to a new awakening. The word *death* is employed in a figurative sense. The theme that man must *"die before he dies"* or that he must be *"born again"* in his present life is taken symbolically, or is commemorated by a ritual.

In this, the candidate has to pass through certain specific experiences (technically termed *"deaths"*). A good example is baptism, which was the main objective at Easter, after Lent, representing *death* of the old self by immersing into water and the rising of the new/renewed self by coming out of the water—as represented by **Horus the Child** rising from the water.

So, back to our triad.

The Father—Ptah represents the divine Architect—the manifester of creation. In the cycle of creation, Sokaris follows Ptah as the second in this Triad. Sokaris represents the darkest point of night—the most inactive point of the deepest stage of the sun's journey beneath the earth.

This darkest point of night is followed by the rise of a new sun.

Nefer-Tum, as the third leg of this triad, represents such a *New Beginning*.

On our life on Earth, the darkest time of year is December 21. This pivotal point of the year was chosen by the

Ancient Egyptians for the annual jubilee of the Ancient Egyptian King, known as the Sed (or Heb-Sed) Festival, which was always held during the month of Kee-hek (Khoiakh, i.e. December) every year, since time immemorial, and continued to be celebrated throughout Ancient Egyptian history.

Such an event is depicted in temples throughout Egypt—but most vividly in Medinet Habu Temple, on the west bank of the River Nile in Luxor. The intent of this annual event was the renewal/rejuvenation of the supernatural powers of the King. The renewal rituals aimed at bringing new life force to the King; i.e. a (figurative) death and a (figurative) rebirth of the reigning King.

As such, this whole process was related and, as such, depicted to be related to the Trinity of Ptah, who descends into Sokaris—the point of figurative death, "to rise again as Nefertum".

For Nefertum represents the perpetual renewal of creation.

———

10.17 NUN/NU/NY

Nun/Nu/Ny represents the unpolarized state of matter. Every Egyptian creation text begins with the same basic concept: that before the beginning of things, there was a liquidy primeval abyss—everywhere, endless, and without boundaries or direction. Egyptians called this cosmic ocean/watery chaos Nun/Nu/Ny.

Scientists agree with the Ancient Egyptian description of

the origin of the universe as being an abyss. Scientists refer to this abyss as neutron soup, where there are neither electrons nor protons—only neutrons forming one huge extremely dense nucleus.

Such chaos, in the pre-creation state, was caused by the compression of matter; i.e. atoms did not exist in their normal states, but were squeezed so closely together that many atomic nuclei were crowded into a space previously occupied by a single normal atom. Under such conditions, the electrons of these atoms were squeezed out of their orbits and move about freely—a degenerate state.

Physically, Nun signifies the watery abyss; the primeval chaos; the ground state of matter from which creation arises. Metaphysically, Nun signifies the subjective being—the symbol of the unformed, undefined, undifferentiated energy/matter, inert or inactive; the uncreated state before the creation.

Egyptian texts state that Nun—the pre-creation chaos—possessed characteristics that were identified with four pairs of primordial powers/forces. Each pair represents the primeval dual-gendered twins—the masculine/feminine aspects. The four pairs are equivalent to the four forces of the universe (the strong force, the weak force, gravity, and electromagnetism).

—————

10.18 OSIRIS (AUSAR, USIRE, ASAR)

Osiris represents the cyclical aspect of nature—the physical creation and its cycles of becoming and returning.

Osiris symbolizes the divine in mortal form. Osiris is usually represented as a mummified, bearded human body wearing the white crown. Osiris is usually depicted carrying:

- the shepherd's crook (being the shepherd of mankind).
- the flail symbolizing the ability to separate wheat from chaff.
- the scepter of supremacy.

Osiris is written with the glyph of the throne and the eye, combining the concepts of legitimacy and divinity. Isis' glyph is the throne/seat and as such she gives her husband Osiris the divine power to rule.

The concept of divine in mortal form is not just limited to human beings. Osiris represents the process, growth, and the underlying cyclical aspects of the universe—in part and as a whole.

We will cover here three main subjects related to Osiris:

1. Osiris in The Creation Process
2. Osiris as 'Our Father in Heaven'
3. Osiris & The Egyptian Resurrection

1.Osiris in The Creation Process

a. The Cyclical Divinity
b. Osiris and Re/Ra
c. Osiris and Isis
d. Osiris the Moon
e. Osiris The Backbone of Creation
f. Osiris The Water—The Four Elements of Creation

1a. The Cyclical Divinity

The main theme of the Ancient Egyptian texts is the cyclical nature of creation being born, living, dying, and regenerating again.

The most obvious and universal cycle to humans is the solar cycle. The sun—born anew each morning – crosses the sky, ages, dies, and travels through the underworld during the night in a cycle of regeneration.

Osiris represents the cyclical aspect of nature—the physical creation and its cycles of becoming and returning.

The universal cyclical number par excellence is SEVEN. Seven of something frequently makes a complete set—the 7 days of the week, 7 colors of the spectrum, 7 notes of the musical scale, etc. The cells of the human body are totally renewed every 7 years.

The Egyptian word for the number seven is *Sab-aa*, which is the same word for *Lion*.

One of Osiris' titles was *The Lion*; the same word as *Seven*.

The zodiac sign of Leo was chosen to signify the time of the year when lions go to the water's edge to drink at the beginning of the rainy season.

Not only is Osiris is related to the number seven and to the Lion, but he is also associated with water supply, as we will see later herein.

Since Osiris represents the latent power of resurrection to begin a new cycle, the Egyptians depicted the deathbed in the shape of a lion being number seven (being Osiris).

Osiris' face is depicted in a black color when representing the *death* state.

And he's shown with a green face when representing the *resurrection/renewal* state.

1b. Osiris and Ra [Re]

Etymologically, the relationship between Re and Osiris becomes self-evident. The Egyptian word for Osiris is Aus-Ra.

The word Aus means the *power of*, or the root of. As such, the name Ausar consists of two parts: Aus-Ra, meaning the power of Ra, meaning the re-birth of Ra [Re].

The principle that makes life come from apparent death is and was called Ausar, who symbolizes the power of renewal. Aus-Ra represents the process, growth, and the underlying cyclical aspects of the universe.

The perpetual cycle of existence—the cycle of life and death—is symbolized by Ra (Re) and Ausar (Osiris). Ra is the living neter [god] who descends into death to become Ausar, the neter [god] of the dead. Ausar [Osiris] ascends and comes to life again as Ra [Re].

The creation is continuous: it is a flow of life progressing towards death. But out of death, a new Ra is born, sprouting new life. Ra is the cosmic principle of energy that moves toward death, and Ausar [Osiris] represents the process of rebirth.

Thus, the terms of life and death become interchangeable: life means slow dying; death means resurrection to new life. The dead person in death is identified with Ausar [Osiris], but he will come to life again, and be identified with Ra [Re].

The perpetual cycle of Ausar [Osiris] and Ra [Re] dominates the Ancient Egyptian texts, such as:

In *The Book of the Coming Forth By Light*, both Ausar and Ra live, die, and are born again. In the Netherworld, the souls of Ausar and Ra meet and are united to form an entity, described so eloquently:

I am His Two Souls in his Twins.

Ra   Ausar

In Chapter 17 of *The Book of the Coming Forth By Light*, the deceased, identified with Ausar[Osiris], says:

> *I am yesterday, I know the morrow.*

In the tomb of Queen Nefertari (wife of Ramses II) is a well-known representation of the dead solar neter (god) as a mummiform body with the head of a ram, accompanied by an inscription, right and left:

> *This is Ra[Re] who comes to rest in Ausar[Osiris].*
> *This is Ausar [Osiris]who comes to rest in Ra[Re].*

1c. Osiris and Isis

Isis represents the female principle in the universe, and her allegorical husband Osiris represents the universal male principle.

The most significant (but not all) aspects of Isis and Osiris are best described by Diodorus of Sicily, *Book I*, 11. 5-6:

> *"These two neteru (gods), they hold, regulate the entire universe, giving both nourishment and increase to all things . . ."*

> *"Moreover, practically all the physical matter which is essential to the generation of all things is furnished by these two neteru* (gods, goddesses), *Isis and Osiris, symbolized as the sun and the moon..."*

Osiris represents the embodiment (emanation) of the moon, reflecting the light of the Isis *The Sunshine*.

1d. Osiris The Moon—Fertility Cycles

Egyptian texts describe Osiris as *The Moon*. The cycle of the moon is the perfect manifestation of the cyclical nature of the universe—in whole and in part. The moon waxes and wanes and then disappears for a few days, to reappear again anew, representing life, death and rebirth—again and again and again.

The principle that makes life come from apparent death was/is called *Ausar* [Osiris], who symbolizes the power of renewal.

Osiris represents the process, growth, and the underlying

cyclical aspects of the universe. Therefore, he was also identified with the spirits (energies) of grain, trees, animals, reptiles, birds, etc.

The most impressive representation of the concept of regeneration, namely Osiris, is the illustration depicting "The Resurrection of the Wheat" with 28 stalks of wheat growing out of his coffin.

("The Resurrection of the Wheat")

The cycle of 28 (7×4) is also the menstruation cycle in women, upon which all human life depends.

It is also interesting to note that Osiris' life (or his reign), according to the symbolic Egyptian Model Story, lasted 28 (7×4) years.

1e. Osiris The Backbone of Creation

The Tet [djed] pillar is the spinal column of creation, which is associated with Osiris as his sacred symbol.

Tet [djed] pillar represents lopped trunk of the cedar tree, symbolizing the possibility of renewed life.

It is depicted here as Osiris' body being surrounded by a cedar tree.

Since the Tet Pillar represents renewed life, it appears (together with the Isis symbol) almost always in all tombs and most (if not all) temples as well as papyri and jewelry.

Isis' symbol was called Thet, which sounds very close to Tet, being the symbol for Osiris.

Isis' Thet is depicted as a knot that appears to be a stylized female genitalia. The Isis amulet conveys the virtue of the blood of Isis, her strength, and her words of power.

Tet [djed] represents the sacrum of Osiris; i.e. the part of the back that is close to the sperm duct, for it symbolized the seed of Osiris. It was, then, natural to depict the genital organs of Isis as a companion amulet; for by the two amulets, the procreative powers of man and women would be symbolized.

1.f. Osiris The Water—The Four Elements of Creation

The four elements of creation represent the four elements necessary to matter.

Osiris represents water as the fertilizing element, fertilizing the soil of Mother Earth—being Isis – to bring forth all creations. Osiris as the water represents the most important cycle in creation; namely, the 'water cycle'.

Egyptians used the four simple phenomena (fire, air, earth and water) to describe the functional roles of the four elements necessary to matter.

The four elements of the world (water, fire, earth, and air), as quoted from Plutarch's *Moralia, Vol. V*:

> *"The Egyptians simply give the name of Osiris to the whole source and faculty creative of moisture, believing this to be the cause of generation and the substance of life-producing seed; and the name of Seth [Typhon] they give to all that is dry, fiery, and arid, in general, and antagonistic to moisture.*
>
> *As the Egyptians regard the Nile as the effusion of*

Osiris, so they hold and believe the earth to be the body of Isis, not all of it, but so much of it as the Nile covers, fertilizing it and uniting with it. From this union they make Horus to be born. The all conserving and fostering Hora, that is the seasonable tempering of the surrounding air, is Horus The insidious scheming and usurpation of Seth [Typhon], then, is the power of drought, which gains control and dissipates the moisture which is the source of the Nile and of its rising".

Here we see how Osiris is representing the water cycle as the fire/heat evaporates the water, which will condensate again and fall as water to the surface of the Earth.

Osiris represents the prospects of inundation and renewed vegetation. Osiris is identified in the Egyptian texts as: **Our Crop** and **Our Harvest**.

2. Our Father in Heaven

a. The Divine in Mortal Form
b. Osiris The Ancestral Spirit
c. Osiris the sacrificial Bull Apis

2a. The Divine in Mortal Form

According to Egyptian philosophy, though all creation is spiritual in origin, man is born mortal but contains within himself the seed of the divine. His purpose in this life is to nourish that seed, and his reward, if successful, is eternal life, where he will reunite with his divine origin.

In order to reunite with our divine origin, the Egyptians followed the allegorical model of Osiris.

According to the Ancient Egyptian traditions, Osiris came to Earth for the benefit of mankind, bearing the title of Manifester of Good and Truth.

As per the Egyptian Model Story, despite his allegorical death, Osiris carried the living seed of eternity—Horus—within him. As such, Osiris represents the mortal man carrying within himself the capacity and power of spiritual salvation. All dead persons were/are equated to Osiris, because Osiris is a cosmic principle, not a historical person.

Let me repeat this fact: **All dead people—males and females—rich and poor—are ALL called Osiris in all funerary texts of all ages**. Every Egyptian's hope was/is for resurrection in a transformed body and for immortality, which could only be realized through the death and resurrection of Osiris.

2b. Osiris the Ancestral Spirit

Ancestors are those people who once lived on Earth and later returned to Heaven. Osiris is the model ancestor—for Osiris once lived (allegorically speaking) on Earth and later returned to Heaven.

The concept of Osiris as the *Grand Ancestor* extended to the Ancient and Baladi Egyptian's entire sociology and existence. From beginning to end, a long chain of ancestral precedents became a custom and a law. Every Egyptian's duty was/is to honor their ancestors with responsible actions and good deeds.

Everything they did – every action, every movement,

every decree – had to be justified in terms of their ancestral precedence to abide by and to explain their actions and deeds.

The Ancient and Baladi Egyptians' entire sociology and existence, from beginning to end, is nothing but a long chain of ancestral precedents—every single link and rivet of which became a custom and a law – from their spiritual fathers unto themselves, in the flesh.

Plato and other writers affirmed the complete adherence of the Egyptians to their own traditions.

Nothing has changed with this attitude since then; for each traveler to Egypt since that time has confirmed the allegiances to such conservatism.

Every Egyptian learned/learns to honor his/her ancestors because s/he will be judged by them—as symbolized in Osiris, the Grand Ancestor, who, as the great judge of the dead, presides over the procedures of the Day of Judgment.

Osiris is always depicted underneath a domed roof.

The dome shape signifies GOLD—the ultimate goal of the spiritual Path.

Like Osiris, ancestors with special spiritual powers—like Saints—are always found buried under a domed small building.

Such domed buildings dot the Egyptian landscape.

More about this point is found in our publication *Egyptian Mystics: Seekers of The Way* by Moustafa Gadalla.

2c. Osiris the sacrificial Bull Apis

[Supporting images for this subsection are to be found in the earlier Apis section of this book chapter.]

It takes a life to save a life. Osiris came to Earth for the benefit of mankind, and was sacrificed and became the Lord of Judgment in the other world. Osiris is the allegorical renewal of life. One must die—figuratively—to be born again.

We find a similar and later conception in the Abraham religion, where Abraham sacrificed a ram to save the life of his son.

One of the most important rituals in the Egyptian annual festivals since ancient times is the ritual sacrifice of the bull, which represents the renewal of the cosmic forces through the death and resurrection of the bull deity.

The Egyptians connected Apis, both living and dead, with Osiris. He was the son of Osiris and was the *"living image of Osiris"*.

After the death of his body, his soul was thought to go to

heaven, where it joined itself to Osiris and formed with him the dual-god Asar-Hepi, or Osiris-Apis. Bull is basically the incarnation of Osiris.

Classical writers of antiquities assert that Apis the bull was sacrificed for Osiris since the time of Mena, 5,000 years ago.

In the Ancient Egyptian traditions, the wine was sacrificed for the blood of Osiris.

Egyptians felt obligated to eat the meat of the sacrificial bull and to drink wine during festivities in order to receive the divine blessing.

That the wine was sacrificed for the blood of Osiris is depicted in practically all Egyptian tombs. The walls of the Ancient Egyptian tombs show vintners pressing new wine, and wine-making is everywhere as a constant metaphor of spiritual processes and the themes of transformation and inner power. The winemaking process of growing, harvesting, pressing and fermenting is a metaphor for spiritual processes.

The soul, or the portion of god within, causes divine ferment in the body of life. It's developed there, as on the vine, by the sun of man's spiritual self. The fermented potency of wine was, at its deepest spiritual level, a symbol of the presence of the incarnated god within the spiritually-aware person.

The tomb occupant is shown here drinking wine—the sacrificial blood of Osiris.

In the *Book of the Dead*, Osiris is addressed as the "Bull of Amentet"; i.e. *"Bull of the Other world"*.

In Ancient Egypt, the Mother deity, Isis, had a son who, in the form of a bull, was sacrificed annually in order to assure the cycle of the seasons and the continuity of Nature.

As per present practices, ancient writers asserted that it was the mother who was chosen to produce a calf with particular qualities—he was The Bull of His Mother, so to speak.

Herodotus, in describing him, says:

> *"Apis, also called Epaphus, is a young bull, whose mother can have no other offspring, and who is reported by the Egyptians to conceive from lightning sent from heaven, and thus to produce the bull-god Apis".*

The religious connotations of this sacrifice are an echo of a sacrifice in the sacrament, where we are reminded of Christ's death so that mankind might be saved. In essence, this is a genuine religious drama in which, as in the Catholic Mass, a god is worshiped and sacrificed.

Diodorus, in *Book I*, [85, 3-5], explains the rejuvenation powers of the sacrificial bull:

> *"Some explain the origin of the honor accorded this bull in this way, saying that at the death of Osiris his soul passed into this animal, and therefore up to this day he always passed into its successors at the times of the manifestation of Osiris."*

Osiris represents the process, growth, and the underlying cyclical aspects of the universe—the principle that makes life come from apparent death.

Osiris represents the rejuvenation/renewal principle in the universe. Therefore, in the Ancient Egypt context, the bull had to suffer a sacrificial death to ensure the life of the community. The sacrifice of the holy animal and the eating of his flesh brought about a state of grace.

Small tablets in Ancient Egyptian tombs sometimes represent a black bull bearing the corpse of a man to its final abode in the regions of the dead. The name of this bull is shown to be Apis, because Osiris represents the state of death in everyone/thing—the divine in mortal form.

Throughout Egypt and in all eras, bulls are depicted in tombs and temples, to be sacrificed during the festivals to renew and to rejuvenate life.

3. Osiris & The Egyptian Resurrection

    a. Like Father Like Son
    b. The Way to The Father
    c. The Glory

3a. Osiris and Horus—Like Father Like Son

In the Egyptian allegory, Osiris' wife Isis was able to conceive her child Horus without Osiris' impregnation. It was the first recorded Immaculate Conception in history.

The Egyptians looked at Osiris and Horus as One, in two complimentary forms.

Likewise, in the Bible teachings, Christ is sometimes referred to as the "Son of God" and at other times simply as God.

In John's Gospel, Christ says: "I and the Father are one."

The Egyptians believed in the anthropomorphic divinity or Horus (Christ) ideal, whose life in this world and the world beyond was typical of the ideal life of man. The chief embodiment of this divinity were Osiris and his son, Horus (Christ).

Neither Osiris nor Horus were ever regarded as historical.

Osiris represents the mortal man carrying within himself the capacity and power of spiritual salvation.

Osiris symbolizes the subconscious—the capacity to act; to do; while Horus symbolizes consciousness, will, and the potential to act; to do.

3b. The Way to The Father

The British Egyptologist, Sir E.A. Wallis Budge, summed it up on page vii of his book, *Osiris and the Egyptian Resurrection*, Vol. I, as follows:

> *"The central figure of the ancient Egyptian religion was Osiris, and the chief fundamentals of his followers were the belief in his divinity, death, resurrection, and absolute control of the destinies of the bodies and souls of men. The central point of each Osirian's religion was his hope of resurrection in a transformed body and*

of immortality, which could only be realized by him through the death and resurrection of Osiris."

From the earliest period of Ancient Egyptian history, the Egyptians believed that Osiris was of divine origin: one partly divine and partly human, who had raised himself from the dead without having seen corruption.

What Osiris had effected for himself, he could effect for man. As a model, the Ancient Egyptians believed that what Osiris did, they could do. Because he had conquered death, the righteous, too, might conquer death and attain everlasting life. They would rise again and attain everlasting life.

The theme in the Egyptian *Book of the Caverns* talks about the necessity for death and dissolution (of the carnal and material), prior to the birth of the spiritual. This is echoed by the biblical Jesus when he says:

Except a corn of wheat fall into the ground and die, it abideth alone: but if it die, it bringeth forth much fruit [John 12:24]

Paul also refers to the same principle in I Corinthians 15:36:

. . . that which thou sowest is not quickened, except it die.

Another example is the biblical wine symbolism, which can be traced to Ancient Egypt, where the walls of the Ancient Egyptian tombs show vintners pressing new wine and wine-making is everywhere a constant metaphor of spiritual processes and the themes of transformation and inner power.

In places in the Egyptian scripts, Osiris himself was characterized as the vine.

The soul, or the portion of god within, causes the divine ferment in the body of life. It's developed there, as on the vine, by the sun of man's spiritual self. The fermented potency of wine was, at its deepest spiritual level, a symbol of the presence of the incarnated God within the spiritually-aware person.

But who do want to be like so that he can guide us back to The Father? The answer is His Son—Horus.

On Judgment Day, Horus, son of Isis, acts as a mediator between the deceased and The Father Osiris. All Egyptians wanted/want *The Son of God* Horus to bring them (dead) to life—as depicted in these Egyptian tombs.

Likewise, in Christianity, the Christian motif was/is based on the need for a mediator; a son of god as an all-powerful shepherd and a begotten savior living among the common man.

3c. The Glory

In the Ancient Egyptian texts, the realized soul achieves glory and joins the Divine Origin. Likewise, the Bible tells us that Jesus is said to have achieved glory only after his death and Resurrection:

> *... God, that raised him up from the dead and gave him glory ...* [I Peter, 1:21]

Glory is the radiant beauty of splendor and magnificence—heaven or the bliss of heaven—which is attained by the highest achievement. Glory is represented in artwork as a halo or a circle of light. In Ancient Egypt, the neter (god) Ra (Re) represents the Light and is depicted as a circle.

———

10.19 PTAH (PHTAS, VULCAN)

In Ancient Egypt, Ptah is/was the Cosmic Architect, the cosmic shaping force, the giver of form (smith). He is/was a patron of crafts, trades, and the arts. He is/was the coagulating, creative fire; simultaneously the cause (of the created world) and effect (of the scission). Ptah is phi, the creative power.

The role of Ptah, as the coagulating fire, is described in the Egyptian *Coffin Texts*, Spell 1130:

> *"I am the Lord of Fire who lives on truth".*

Ptah represents the manifestation of the cosmic words of Ra (Re), as spoken by Thoth, in accordance with the laws of balance and equilibrium—Ma-at. Therefore, Ptah sits enthroned or stands upon a pedestal, which is in the form of the glyph for Maat, to emphasize the importance of balancing energies in the transformation process, from a raw to finished form.

Creation is the sorting out (by giving definition to bringing order to all the chaos) of the undifferentiated energy matter and consciousness of the primeval state, where we have a highly condensed energy in the pre-creation state, Nun. We also have the prime mover of inert energy in creation, which is symbolized by the Divine Sound—Thoth. In the orderly sequence of creation, the next stage is to give shapes and forms to the constituents of the orderly created word. In the orderly sequence of creation, the release of the inert energy needs to be controlled and managed so as to provide a well-formed, orderly creation.

The role of Ptah's "sons" on Earth—being the artisans/ craftsmen – is found, appropriately enough, in Stanza 40 of the Ancient Egyptians' Leiden Papyrus J 350, which introduces the 'Becoming', telling of the Divine Craftsman of the universe, symbolized as Ptah.

Ptah is/was the patron of crafts, trades, and the arts. Ptah's counterparts on Earth are the smiths, who were/ are highly revered and sometimes feared because of their supernatural powers in handling, controlling, and manipulating the four elements of creation. These four elements are always present at the smith's forge: fire, the air of the bellows to tease fire, water to tame fire, and Earth, as the provider of raw materials.

Blacksmiths are/were highly revered and sometimes feared because they are believed to be powerful magicians, and their work was shrouded in mysticism. Blacksmiths had a closed and secret society through which their skills were/are passed from one generation to another. The Pharaoh himself, as well as other spiritual leaders and intermediaries, were/are identified with the mysterious craft of the smith.

Ptah's counterparts on Earth (the smiths) perform the work aimed at shaping the environments and the individuals around them. Their activities include those of technicians, healers, sorcerers, and mediators.

The society relied on these artisans to be their intermediaries to guide their religious upbringing, such as boys' circumcision and training. They also helped the rest of society to solve their problems, from the physical (e.g. fixing tools) to the metaphysical (e.g. influencing future events).

Ptah's depictions and shrines are found all over Egypt, such as Thebes/Luxor, Abydos, Abu Simbel, and Memphis.

Ptah—like many other neteru—functions alone but is often associated with other neteru (gods/goddesses) to form composites or triads.

—————

10.20 RE [RA]

Re (Ra) represents the primeval, cosmic, creative force. The Ancient Egyptian text, known as *The Litany of Re*, describes Re as:

> **The One Joined Together, Who Comes Out of His Own Members.**

The Ancient Egyptian definition of Re is 'the perfect representation that the Unity (whole universe) is the sum of the many diverse entities'.

Creation is the sorting out (giving definition to/bringing order to) of all the chaos (the undifferentiated energy/matter and consciousness) of Nun—the primeval state. Ra (Re) represents this primeval creative force, which causes the transformation of Nun from its undifferentiated state to differentiated energy/matter (things, objects, thoughts, forces, physical phenomena). Accordingly, all of the Ancient Egyptian accounts of creation exhibit well-defined, clearly demarcated stages.

We will be covering the following subjects as they relate to Re [Ra]:

1. Re in The Creation Process
2. The Creation Cycle

1. Re in The Creation Process

    a. In The Beginning—Nun
    b. Atam
    c. Re: The Manifested Atam—Atam-Re
    – Re: Twin Definitions

– Orderly creation Process
d. Isis: The Female Re
e. Re's "secret" name
f. Re is NOT The Sun
g. Re as Khepri, The Beetle
h. Re, Logos of Thoth–"Mouth of Re"
i. Re and The Big Bang
j. Re's 75 Manifestations

1a. In The Beginning—Nun

So what is Re? Where did it (not a he or a she; but both) come from?

So, as always, you go back to square one, so to speak—the point of beginning. Every Egyptian creation text begins with the same basic belief that before the beginning of things, there was a liquidy primeval abyss—everywhere, dark, endless, and without boundaries or directions. Egyptians called this cosmic ocean/watery chaos Nun, meaning non-existence. It is the Nothingness that is the source of Every Thing.

1b.Atam

Atam is the totality of the orderly energy matrix during the creation stage, while Nun is the disorderly energy compound—the Subjective Being. The total divine energy within the universe is called Nun in its chaotic state and Atam in its orderly creation and its point of state/process.

1c. Re: The Manifested Atam—Atam-Re

Atam represents the realization of the total cosmic existence. In the Egyptian text, Atam states:

"I appeared as Re on the eastern horizon of heaven . . ."

Another version in this ancient Egyptian book reads:

I am Atam (the All) when I was alone in the Watery Abyss.
I am Re in his manifestations . . .

Re represents the primeval, cosmic, creative force—the manifestation of Atam.

When Atam is combined with Re (the creative force), the result is Re-Atam, representing the manifestation of the creative force.

Re-Atam is depicted in human form—Symbol of the Universe—carrying the ankh (life) and the scepter (creative power).

Re represents the primeval, cosmic, creative force. The Ancient Egyptian text, known as *The Litany of Re*, describes Re as:

The One Joined Together, Who Comes Out of His Own Members.

The Ancient Egyptian definition of Re is the perfect representation that the Unity (whole universe) is the sum of the many diverse entities.

1d. Isis: The Female Re

The Ancient Egyptian texts describe Isis as being:

The Light-giver in heaven with Re.

Isis, then, is the emanated energy from the Total one. As the female principle in the universe, only she can conceive and deliver the created universe.

In other words, Isis is the Image of the cosmic creative impulse recognized by the term Re. Thus, when speaking of Re, the ancient Egyptian text says:

"Thou art the bodies of Isis."...

This implies that Re, the creative energy, appears in the different aspects of the cosmic female principle Isis. As such, Isis is recognized as:

"The female Re".

1e. Re's "secret" name

The traditional story of the Mystery of the Divine Name is found on an Ancient Egyptian papyrus now in the Turin Museum.

In the story, Re refused to tell even the most beloved Being, Isis, his real (secret) name.

The events of the story end with Re "divulging" his *"secret"* name as *Amen*.

It should be noted that *Amen* means secret/hidden. In other words, under all difficult circumstances, Re (as a model for all) did not divulge his real name, but only stated that his secret name was [Amen]—meaning SECRET; same as SACRED.

1f. Re is NOT The Sun

The solar energy of the sun is only one of numerous manifestations of Re. That Re is not just the sun (only a singular form) was also confirmed in the following verse from the Story of Re and Isis, in which Re states:

"I have multitude of names, and multitude of forms".

The *Litany of Re* describes SEVENTY-FIVE of these forms

1g. Re as Khepri The Beetle

Re is frequently represented as a large black scarab beetle sitting in the solar boat and rolling the sun disc; or as a man whose human head is replaced by a scarab beetle.

As such, Re must be the original divine scarab. The Egyptian name for the scarab beetle was Khepri; a multiple word meaning 'he who brings into being'.

Re is described in the *Unas Funerary (Pyramid) Texts*:

"They cause thee to come into being as Re, in his name of Khepri".

Horapollo Niliaeus explains the symbolism of the scarab in this way:

"To signify the only begotten, or birth, or a father, or the world, or man, they [Egyptians] draw a scarab. The only begotten, because this animal is self-begotten, unborn of the female. For its birth takes place only in the following way. When the male wishes to have offspring, it takes some cow-dung and makes a round ball of it, very much in the shape of the world. Rolling it

*with its hind legs from east to west, it faces the east,
so as to give it the shape of the world, for the world is
borne from the east to the west."*

In the elaborate symbolism of the transformational
(funerary) texts, the dead person, identified with Osiris,
passed through analogous stages in the night of the
underworld and was reborn as a new Re, in his form of
Khepri (the scarab beetle), in the morning. The analogy to
the sun—disappearing at night and appearing in glory in
the morning—is clear. The scarab was the symbol of the
transforming quality of the sun; the light that becomes
out of darkness.

1h. Re Logos of Thoth

The Egyptian texts state that the created universe came
out of the mouth (of Re), and the mouth is the symbol of
Unity—the One—in hieroglyphs.

The creation process (i.e. transformation [differentia-
tion]) is achieved through sound (the Word) as the prime
mover of the inert energy.

Egyptian creation texts repeatedly stress the belief of creation by the Word. It was Thoth who uttered the words,
commanded by Re, that created the world. In the Egyptian *Book of the Coming Forth by Day* (wrongly translated as
the *Book of the Dead*), the oldest written text in the world,
we read:

>*"I am the Eternal...I am that which created the
Word...I am the Word..."*

1i. Re's 75 Manifestations

Creation is the sorting out of (giving definition to/bringing order to) all the chaos (the undifferentiated energy/matter and consciousness) of Nun—the primeval state. Ra (Re) represents this primeval creative force, which causes the transformation of Nun from its undifferentiated state to differentiated energy/matter (things, objects, thoughts, forces, physical phenomena). Accordingly, all of the Ancient Egyptian accounts of creation exhibit well defined, clearly-demarcated stages.

The *Litany of Re* describes the demarcated aspects of the creative principle being recognized as the neteru (gods/goddesses), whose actions and interactions in turn created the universe.

As such, all the Egyptian neteru (gods/goddesses) who took part in the creation process are aspects of Re.

There are 75 forms or aspects of Re. As such, Re is often incorporated into the names of other neteru (gods/goddesses) such as in Amen-Re, Re-Atum, Re-Harakhti, etc.

The composition of this Litany can be found at the entrance to some of the royal ancient tombs. In it, the king addresses the seventy-five forms of Re by their names.

Each recited name represents a specific aspect/attribute of Re.

These names are not just labels. In ancient Egypt, a name was like a short resume or synopsis of the qualities of the neter/person/principle/animal. Here is an excerpt from the Litany, translated by the Egyptologist Piankoff:

"Homage to thee, Re, supreme power, Lord of the Caverns, with hidden forms, he who goes to rest into the mysteries when he transforms (himself) into Deba of The One Who Joined Together!

Homage to thee, Re, supreme power, this Becoming One who folds his wings, he who goes to rest in the Netherworld, and transforms (himself) into He Who Comes Out of His Own Members!

Homage to thee, Re, supreme power, Exalted Earth, who gives birth to his neteru, he who protects what is in him, He who transforms (himself) into He at the Head of His Cavern"

2. The Creation cycle

    a. The Circle Symbol of Re
    b. The Creation Cycle Dual—RA and aus-RA
    c. The Re Eye of Enlightenment

2a. The Circle Symbol of Re

The cosmic creative force, Ra (Re), is written as a circle with a dot or point in the center. It is a circle moving in a circle; one and solitary. The circle symbolically represents the Absolute, or undifferentiated, Unity. The circle, appropriately enough, is the universal archetype of creation.

The Circle of Ra represents:

    – at the center—the cause/nothingness
    – along the circumference—effect/manifestation

2b. The Creation Cycle Dual [RA and aus-RA]

The perpetual cycle of existence—the cycle of life and death—is symbolized by Ra (Re) and Ausar (Osiris). Ra is the living neter who descends into death to become Ausar, the neter of the dead. Ausar ascends and comes to life again as Ra. The creation is continuous: it is a flow of life progressing towards death. But out of death, a new Ra is born, sprouting new life.

The relationship between the cycle of death and resurrection is reflected in the "name" of Ausar, which consists of two syllables—Aus-Ra.

The first syllable of the name (Aus-Ra) is pronounced Aus or Us, meaning *"strength, might, power"*.

Aus – RA then means 'the strength or source of the RA'.

Ra is the cosmic principle of energy that moves toward death, and Ausar represents the process of rebirth. Thus, the terms of life and death become interchangeable: life means slow dying, death means resurrection to new life. The dead person in death is identified with Ausar, but he will come to life again, and will be identified with Ra.

The perpetual cycle of Ausar and Ra dominates the Ancient Egyptian texts.

In Chapter 17 of *The Book of the Coming Forth By Light*, the deceased, identified with Ausar, says:

I am yesterday, I know the morrow.

In the tomb of Queen Nefertari (wife of Ramses II) is a

well-known representation of the dead solar neter (god) as a mummiform body with the head of a ram, accompanied by an inscription, right and left:

This is Ra who comes to rest in Ausar.
This is Ausar who comes to rest in Ra.

The *Litany of Ra* is basically a detailed amplification of a short passage of Chapter 17 of *The Book of the Coming Forth by Light,* describing the merging of Ausar and Ra into a Twin Soul.

2c. The Re's Eye of Enlightenment

The most distinctive Egyptian symbol is the eye, which plays many complex and subtle roles. The eye is the part of the body able to perceive the light, and is therefore a symbol for the spiritual ability. This is equated to the Gospels, *"those with eyes to see"*.

— — — — —

10.21 RE HOR AKHTI [RAHORACHTY]

Re-Hor.Akhti is one of the 75 manifestations of Re.

Re-Hor-akhti represents the renewed creation process—a matured and a renewed Horus.

Horus represents the realized divine principle—the goal of all initiated teachings.

As shown earlier under 'Horus', Hor.Akhti is the last stage in the process of spiritualization, that signifies the renewal/new beginning. This will be manifested in the form of Re-Hor.Akhti—a new—or better yet—A Renewed Creation.

Hor-akhti is, then, a new Alpha usually depicted in green, the color of rejuvenation.

As such, Hor-Akhti is shown as the head or Foreman of the Jury on Judgment Day scenes.

Re-Hor.Akhti is depicted in mainly three forms that corresponds to each's function, as follows:

a. The Human-Headed Lion—Sphinx

Similar to the depiction of a bird headed man of the Ba, we have the Sphinx, a man-headed lion.

The Sphinx represents Horus on the horizon—Hor-Akhti.

This renewed Horus in Giza is Facing the east, welcoming a new sun everyday

b. The Green Falcon-Headed Human

The green falcon-headed human represents the spiritualization capacity and potential in all of us, as humans.

c. The Cosmic Green Falcon

The Pure form of a falcon represents the Cosmic principle of spiritualization and renewal—being green.

Also see both Horus and Re, in this chapter.

———

10.22 RESHPU (RESHEF, RESHEPH)

Reshpu (Reshef) represents wilderness and travel. As such, Reshpu (Reshef) appears unshaven, as per the Ancient Egyptian custom of not shaving while traveling.

The tradition of the unshaven Egyptian traveler was well recognized by classical Greek and Roman writers such as Diodorus, who wrote in his *Book I*, [2]:

> *"And when all his [travel] preparations had been completed Osiris made a vow to the gods that he would let his hair grow until his return to Egypt and then made his way through Ethio pia; and this is the reason why this custom with regard to their hair was observed among the Egyptians until recent times, and why those who journeyed abroad let their hair grow until their return home".*

This is the reason that some male deities are shown with beards and long hair—not because they are "Syrians", but because they are traveling Egyptians. Such unshaven representation of male deities will be naturally found in shrines and temples outside Egypt proper, because that is where the travel occurs.

Reshpu (Reshef) is identified with Menu (Min), who represents prosperity.

Also see Hathor/Astarte, in the next chapter of this book.

——————

10.23 SEBEK (SOBEK, SUCHOS)

As a crocodile-headed deity, Sebek (Sobek, Suchos) represents the end of a cycle—death. Without death, there can be no possibility of a return to the source.

Etymologically, (Sebek or, more correctly, *Sabaq)* means *Former.* The Egyptian word for crocodile is Te- MSaHh. Its verb form is MaSaHh, which means 'to *rub/anoint'.*

The English word Messiah originated also from the Hebrew and Aramaic Mashih which, in its form as a verb, MeSHeH., means 'to anoint'. This word is of Egyptian origin, where MeSSeH [the letters in Egyptian are equivalent to sh in Hebrew and Aramaic] signified the ritual of anointing Ancient Egyptian Kings with the fat of crocodiles, as was the tradition with all kings in Ancient Egypt since at least 2700 BCE.

Anointing was a ritual of the coronation of the Egyptian King. Thus, the Christ/Messiah means 'the anointed one', who is the king.

The concept of the birth of the Messiah without sexual intercourse originated in Ancient Egypt. Isis is said to have conceived her son Horus after her husband Osiris' death.

The cosmic force responsible for her impregnation was MeSSeH, the crocodile star, as per Spell 148 of the *Coffin Texts*:

> *"The crocodile star (MeSSeH) strikes ... Isis wakes pregnant with the seed of Osiris*—namely Horus".

(Horus resulting from the strike of the crocodile star.)

The cause of impregnation, Sebeq, sits between the Virgin Mother and her Child.

[Much more information is to be found under 'Crocodile 'in the previous chapter.]

─────

10.24 SETH (SET, SUTEKH, TYPHON)

Seth (Set) represents the universal role of opposition in all aspects of life both physically and metaphysically.

The Ancient Egyptians had a very enlightening view on what people call the "devil" or "Satan".

Seth, for the Egyptians, is basically a necessary evil. Seth is an important aspect of creation.

We will be covering, here, the role of Seth in the following areas:

1. The Creation Cycle
2. Lord of Wilderness
3. Seth and Horus—The Inner Struggle

1. The Creation Cycle

For Ancient Egyptians, the initial act of creation caused the division of the original unity. This breaking up created multiplicity, which resulted in the various elements of the world. This break-up, by its nature, is an opposition of the original unity.

Seth represents this power of opposition; however, without opposition there can be no creation. As such, Seth is an important force, because opposition is an essential aspect of creation and its continuance.

The world as we know it—from the smallest particle to the largest planet—is kept in balance by a law that is based on the balanced dual nature of all things. Without the balance between two opposing forces, there would be no creation; i.e. no universe. For example, the galaxies are mainly subjected to two opposing forces:

– The expulsion forces, resulting from the effect of the Big Bang.
– The gravity forces, which pull the galaxies together.

The lack of one of these two forces will cause the galaxies to either spin out of control or collapse into each other.

Seth symbolizes one of the four elements of solidity/stability of the universe; namely fire/heat, as mentioned in Plutarch's *Moralia Vol. V*:

> *"The Egyptians simply give the name of ... Seth [Typhon] ... to all that is dry, fiery, and arid, in general, and antagonistic to moisture."*

Without fire/heat, the universe cannot exist. Also, being "antagonistic to moisture" is essential in the water cycle of evaporation, condensation, etc.

2. Lord of Wilderness

Seth is associated with the desert/waste/wilderness areas and their associated animals, such as the immense coiled serpent, the black pig, and the ass. Each animal symbolizes a different aspect.

Seth is depicted as a human figure with the head of an unidentified animal. Seth is also depicted as an animal with a forked tail.

3. Seth and Horus—The Inner Struggle

Seth, represented as the ass, symbolizes the ego. The supreme obstacle for the human being is his own egotistic consciousness that is dominated by pride, egotism, and the self-centered greed and lust of Seth.

The symbolic Ancient Egyptian scene shows Horus and his four disciples, each armed with a knife, demonstrating to Osiris their success in controlling the ego. Their success is symbolized by the ass-headed man (a symbol of the ego in man) with knives stuck in his body and bound by his arms to the forked stick.

The archetypal inner struggle in the Egyptian model is symbolized in the struggle between Horus and Seth. It is the archetypal struggle between opposing forces. Horus, in this context, is the divine man, born of nature, who must do battle against Seth, his own kin, representing the power of opposition (and not evil, in the narrow sense). Seth represents the concept of opposition in all aspects of life (physically and metaphysically).

We must continuously learn and evolve, like Horus—whose name means *He Who is Above*. In other words, we must strive to reach higher and higher.

We learn and act by affirmation of the *Horus* in each of us, and by negating the *Seth* within us. The obstacles within each of us, represented by Seth, must be controlled and/ or overcome. Such obstacles are the ego, laziness, overconfidence, arrogance, evasiveness, indifference, etc.

In the Egyptian model, Seth represents the wilderness

and foreign aspects within each of us. It is therefore that in Ancient Egyptian temples, tombs, and texts, human vices are depicted as foreigners (the sick body is sick because it is/was invaded by foreign germs). Foreigners are depicted as subdued—arms tightened/tied behind their backs—to portray inner self-control.

The most vivid example of self-control is the common depiction of the Pharaoh (The Perfected Man) on the outer walls of Ancient Egyptian temples, subduing/controlling foreign enemies—the enemies (impurities) within.

— — — — —

10.25 SOKARIS (SOKAR, SAKAR, SEQR)

Sokaris represents the farthest point of a cycle like the darkest point of night—the most inactive point of the deepest stage of the sun's journey beneath the Earth.

Sokaris is described as the "neter of the necropolis."

Saqqara (named after Saqar) was a prominent cemetery site in Ancient Egypt, since (and probably prior to) the time of dynastic Egypt.

Sokaris is depicted as falcon-headed deity. Actually, Saqar or Ssaqar means *falcon* in the Egyptian tongue.

Sokaris is usually combined with Ptah and/or Osiris in binary form; i.e. Ptah–Sokaris or Sokaris-Osiris.

Sokaris is also associated with several triads such as the triad Ptah–Sokaris–Nefertum, The Father, Son and Holy Spirit.

See Nefertum, above, in this chapter, for more details about this trinity.

————————

10.26 SHU

Shu signifies the void, space or extension. Shu is usually depicted as a male, bearded divinity wearing the ostrich feather of Ma-at (cosmic law) upon his head.

Shu is closely associated with Tefnut—being a pair/dual Tefnut- and is the female counterpart and twin of Shu. Tefnut is usually shown as a female figure with the head of a lioness, wearing the solar disk, uraeus, or both. Tefnut is associated with moisture.

More about the dual/pair Shu and Tefnut in the next two chapters of this book.

Shu is commonly depicted in creation scenes of standing and supporting, with his hands, the outstretched body of Nut.

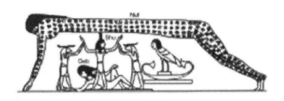

— — — — —

10.27 THOTH [TEHUTI, HERMES, MERCURY]

Thoth represents the intermediary link between the metaphysical and the physical worlds. Thoth represents the power of sound (the Word) as the prime mover of inert energy.

Egyptian creation texts repeatedly stress the belief of creation by the Word. In the *Egyptian Book of the Coming Forth by Day* (wrongly translated as the *Book of the Dead*), the oldest written text in the world, we read:

> *"I am the Eternal...I am that which created the Word ... I am the Word..."*

The Word means action. In human terms, we say, "A man of his word," which signifies the action behind the word.

The Egyptian texts state that the created universe came out of the mouth (of Re), and the mouth is the symbol of Unity—the One—in hieroglyphs. The creation process, i.e. transformation (differentiation), is achieved through sound (the Word) as the prime mover of the inert energy.

In effect, The Supreme contained the potential existence of all things, and when He spoke, He and all things with Him came into objective existence.

As the link between the extra-human and the terrestrial, Thoth moved, like Mercury (his equivalent), at immense speed, negating time and space in the same way that inner experience does.

In Ancient Egyptian traditions, the words of Ra (Re), revealed through Thoth, became the things and creatures of this world; i.e. the words (meaning sound energies) created the forms in the universe.

As such, Thoth represents the link between the metaphysical (extra-human) and the physical (terrestrial).

As such, Thoth represents the crack of dawn and therefore is related to the baboon.

Ground zero of the creation cycle was/is the crucial moment of sunrise. The Ancient Egyptians were fascinated by this point of beginning.

The baboon emits a crackling sound at the crack of dawn—The Point of beginning.

The baboon represents this point of beginning extremely well. The baboon is almost human and, as such, it represents this crucial moment that precedes the awakening of the sun. The baboon represents this state in humans just before they gain consciousness—the awakening.

Thoth is portrayed as an ibis-headed male figure, or sometimes as all ibis. Thoth is also associated with the baboon, representing the spirit of dawn and ground zero in the creation process.

Thoth is often depicted with a crescent moon.

Thoth is also referred to as the Divine Tongue who gave names to the divine beings that resulted from the Big Bang. As such, Thoth represents spoken/written language, knowledge, etc.

Several of Thoth's attributes were confirmed by Diodorus of Sicily:

> *"It was by Thoth [Hermes], according to Ancient Egyptians, that the common language of mankind was first further articulated, and that many objects which were still nameless received an appellation, that the alphabet were defined, and that ordinances regarding the honors and offerings due to the neteru* (gods, goddesses)*were duly established; he was the first also to observe the orderly arrangement of the stars and the*

harmony of the musical sounds and their nature."
Book I, Section 16-1

——

Some neteru (gods/goddesses) represent specific aspects of the intellectual powers of Thoth, as shown below.

From the earliest times, Egypt has been celebrated for its magicians, and accounts of their marvelous achievements have been documented not only in Ancient Egyptian records, but also in the Bible and in the works of several of the classical writers. Furthermore, many of the tales in the famous collection of stories known as The Arabian Nights show what wonder-working powers were attributed to magicians in medieval Egypt.

Heka [shown herein] represents the Ancient Egyptian magical power of words. He is usually depicted holding two snakes with total ease.

Heka is a member of a triad representing specific aspects of the intellectual powers of Thoth. It is the trinity of HuSia-Heka.

Hu represents the authoritative utterance. Hu is complemented by Sia (consciousness).

Sia represents the mind (or consciousness), knowledge, understanding, perception, etc. **Sia** is complemented by **Hu** (authoritative utterance).

Heka represents the ability to transform by using the right words. Therefore, Heka is identified with both Sia and Hu.

As such, Hu–Sia–Heka represents a trinity of active transformation.

The right words have powerful transformational (magical) effects. The words of power (magical words) are called Heka-u (plural of Heka).

— -

The Egyptians have never ever accredited a source of any type of knowledge to a mortal. The Divine is the ONLY source. As such, all references are made to Thoth—The Divine Intellect.

Clement Alexandrinus (200 CE) told us of 42 volumes associated with Thoth's domain, which include:

- Four books about astronomy—one containing a list of the fixed stars, a second on the phenomena of the sun and moon, and two others on the rising of the stars.

- Several books about cosmography and geography, the course of the sun, moon, and the five planets, the chorography of Egypt and scheme of the Nile, and an account of the supplies of the temples and the lands apportioned to them, touching on measures and the requisites of sacred things.

- Two books on music.

- Six books on medicine.

- Ten books were dedicated to the honors to be rendered to the neteru (gods/goddesses) and other actions of Egyptian piety, such as sacrifices, first-fruits, vows, ceremonies, feasts, and similar things.

- Ten books about the laws of the country and of the neteru (gods/goddesses) and the instruction of the priests.

- A book about the instruction of youth.

—–

As a mediator, Thoth is always depicted striding actively

while recording in writing the various actions and deeds—such as in the typical Judgment Day scene.

—–

The netert [goddess] Seshat is closely associated with Thoth, and is considered to be a female counterpart of Thoth.

More about Seshat in the next chapter of this book.

CHAPTER 11 : MOST COMMON FEMALE HUMAN FORMS DIVINITIES

In a previous chapter we explained the choice of a human body as a symbol of the universe and how the Egyptian differentiated between earthly and universal human images. In order for creation to exist and to be maintained, this divine energy must be thought of in terms of male and female principles. Therefore, Ancient Egyptians expressed the cosmic energy forces in the terms of netert (female principle) and neter (male principle).

We also discussed earlier animal symbolism. The animal-headed human images represent the divine forces which the Egyptian called Neteru. They are the manifestation of the divine energy in the universe.

Each deity will be explained with a very brief review of each's metaphysical functions/attributes, to help stay away from silly descriptions and focus on the REAL subtle/deep meanings. It is always helpful to think of 'figures of speech' related to each image, to recognize each's nature/behavior/characteristics/attributes.

It is worth repeating that the primary function of these Egyptian Ideograms is to represent thoughts. This means that one must be searching for both the Figurative (an object stands for one of its qualities) and the Allegorical (an object is linked through enigmatic conceptual processes).

We must always keep in mind the relationships between visual forms and their meaning. A visual form may be mimetic or imitative, directly copying the features of the object it represents; it may be associative, suggesting attributes which are not visually present, such as abstract properties incapable of literal depiction; and finally, it may be symbolic, meaningful only when decoded according to conventions or systems of knowledge which, though not inherently visual, are communicated through.

>>> It should be noted that the digital edition of this book as published in PDF and E-book formats has a substantial number of photographs that compliment the text materials throughout this chapter.

In this chapter, we will show the most common female forms for the Egyptian divinities/neteru. We have arranged it here in an alphabetical order, using the most recognized names for such deities for the English-speaking peoples, followed by other [grammatical] varied forms of each deity.

We begin with Isis being the female principle of creation and then her female manifestations in other 'deities', in alphabetical order.

11.1 ISIS (AUSET, AST)—THE DIVINE FEMALE PRINCIPLE/PRINCIPAL

11.1a. Her Name

The present-day common use of the name *Isis* is limited to her aspect of maternal devotion, fidelity and tenderness. But she is much more than that—she represents the divine female principle that includes the creative power that conceived—both physically and metaphysically—and brought forth all living creatures.

The Ancient Egyptians looked at Isis as the symbol of the cosmic feminine principle. This principle encompasses thousands of the feminine qualities and attributes and the Egyptians had names to describe each manifestation of this feminine principle.

In the culture of English-speaking peoples, a name is merely a label to distinguish someone or something from another. But for the Egyptians, both the ancient and present-day silent majority, a common name represents the resume or synopsis of the qualities and attributes of an entity. Egyptian common names are the attributes and qualities of any entity. This will be similar to the English language words for carpenter, farmer, etc., which represent a specific activity and not merely meaningless names.

In the English language, we refer to her name as Isis; but the Egyptians had a name that recognizes the totality of her cosmic feminine principle. This all-encompassing Egyptian word is *Auset*. So what is in this Ancient Egyptian name? Let us look at the meanings of Auset, to demonstrate how a name represents qualities and attributes.

Auset consists of the main word Aus and the suffix et. Aus means the source; the power. In mathematics, we say

2 to the power of 2. This mathematical power is called Aus. The suffix 'et' at the end of Aus-et is a feminine ending.

Back to Aus…in addition to meaning 'the source' and 'the power', it also means 'the origin, the cause'.

In this regard, we will show Auset to be the source, power, and cause of the created universe, inclusive of everything within this universe.

Another interesting meaning of Au-set is **The Lady**, and indeed, she is the Lady of Heaven and Earth. She represents the feminine principle in the universe. This principle manifests itself in different forms and ways, and therefore Isis was called by the Ancient Egyptians as *Auset of the 10,000 Names (meaning, attributes)*.

Several words are derived directly from the Egyptian name Auset, such as *Seta*, which means the number 6. This is very significant because 6 is the ultimate number of space, volume, and time. The cube with its six surfaces is the model of Earth, or the material world, and in Ancient Egypt, Auset represents the womb that contains creation within. As such, she represents the universe's womb as well as Earth; as we will discuss in detail, later.

Another related meaning to the name Auset is the English word '*seat*'. Isis is portrayed as always wearing a seat or throne on her head to symbolize her as the source of legitimacy, which is manifested in the Ancient Egyptian (as well as the present-day silent majority) adherence to the matrilineal and matriarchal society [more about it in

Egyptian Cosmology: The Animated Universe by Moustafa Gadalla].

As we have noted, the use of the common name (in the English language) of Isis hinders our comprehension of valuable information, knowledge, and wisdom. However, to make it easier for the English-speaking reader, we will continue to use the word Isis and other Ancient Egyptian names familiar to the English language reader.

The role of Isis as the divine female principle in the Creation process has been recognized by all. She exists everywhere and is known to all, since time immemorial.

Plutarch made note of that in his *Moralia Vol. V*:

> **"Isis is, in fact, the female principle of Nature, and is receptive of every form of generation, and by most people has been called by countless names, since, because of the force of Reason. she turns herself to this thing or that and is receptive of all manner of shapes and forms."**

To appreciate the roles of Isis as the female principle of nature, we must find her primary cosmic role in the orderly sequence of the Creation of the universe.

11.1b. The Universal Womb

The expanding universe, resulting from the Big Bang, is like a huge bubble—or better yet, it is a type of womb that contains the whole universe. This expanding universe is the womb that contains all creation. This is the womb of Isis—the universal mother of all.

Creation occurs when divine energy is Born in a type of a womb...which is represented by Isis. The womb has several manifestations. On the universal level, it is the space that contains the universe. It is also the womb of the mother or the seeds planted in the soil: all these manifestations of the womb represent Isis.

11.1c. Isis: The Image of Atam

We have seen how an orderly creation—in the form of Atam, *the Complete One*—emerged out of the pre-creation chaotic state of the Nun—the nothingness. We have also seen how one state of being develops or emerges into the next state of being, and how every two consecutive stages are images of each other. Nun and Atam are images of each other, like the numbers 0 and 1. 0 is 'nothing, nil'; and 1 means 'the all'.

The first thing that developed from the light of unity of the Complete One was *the force of Active Reason* as 'He' made two arise from one, by repetition.

This divine active reason/thought is the first 'thing' of which existence may proceed as the act, offspring, and image of the first—Atam. The ability to conceive—both mentally and physically—was naturally represented by the female principle—Isis being the feminine side of

Atam's unity. This was confirmed plainly in Plutarch's writings where he wrote, in his *Moralia Vol. V*:

"..., since, because of the force of Reason. Isis turns herself to this thing or that and is receptive of all manner of shapes and forms."

It is Isis being this Divine-Mind, Divine-Intellection, or Divine-Intellectual-Principle that begins the existence of Plurality or Complexity or Multiplicity.

The relationship between the master of the universe—The Complete One—and the mother of creation is best described in musical terms. The relationship between Atam—the Complete One—and his female image (being Isis) is like the relationship between the sound of a note and its octave note. Consider a string of a given length as unity. Set it vibrating; it produces a sound. Stop the string at its midpoint and set it vibrating. The frequency of vibrations produced is double that given by the whole string, and the tone is raised by one octave. The string length has been divided by two; and the number of vibrations per second has been multiplied by two: one half (1:2) has created its mirror opposite (2:1), 2/1. This harmonic relationship is represented by Atam and Isis.

Isis' number is two, which symbolizes the power of multiplicity: the female mutable, receptacle, horizontal, representing the basis of everything. In the Ancient Egyptian thinking, Isis as the number two is the image of the first principle—the divine intellect.

11.1d. Isis: The Female Re

The relation of the intellect to the Complete One, Atam, is like the relation of the light of the sun effusing from the sun. The Ancient Egyptian texts describe Isis as being the divine sunshine, for she is called:

> *The daughter of the universal Lord.*
> *The female Re.*
> *The Light-giver in heaven with Re.*

Isis, then, is the emanated energy from the Complete One. As the female principle in the universe, only she can conceive and deliver the created universe. In other words: Isis is the image of the cosmic creative impulse, recognized by the term Re. Thus, when speaking of Re, the Ancient Egyptian text says:

> *"Thou art the bodies of Isis."*

This implies that Re, the creative energy, appears also in the different aspects of the cosmic female principle Isis. As such, Isis is recognized as:

> *The female Re.*
> *The Lady of the beginning of time.*
> *The prototype of all beings.*
> *The greatest of the neteru—[meaning the divine forces].*
> *The Queen of all the neteru.*

Isis is recognized in the Ancient Egyptian texts as the God-Mother. How loving Isis is—our God-Mother. She—the female principle—is the matrix of the created universe. Matrix is a *motherly* term, being *mater-x*.

11.1e. Isis and Osiris

Isis represents the female principle in the universe and her allegorical husband Osiris represents the universal male principle.

The most significant (but not all) aspects of Isis and Osiris are best described by Diodorus of Sicily, *Book I*, 11. 5-6:

> *"These two neteru (gods), they hold, regulate the entire universe, giving both nourishment and increase to all things . . . .*
>
> *Moreover, practically all the physical matter which is essential to the generation of all things is furnished by these two neteru (gods), Isis and Osiris, symbolized as the sun and the moon. The sun contributing the fiery element and the spirit, the moon the wet and the dry, and both together the air; and it is through these elements that all things are engendered and nourished. And so it is out of the sun and moon that the whole physical body of the universe is made complete; and as for the five parts just named of these bodies—the spirit, the fire, the dry, as well as the wet, and, lastly, the air-like—just as in the case of a man we enumerate head and hands and feet and the other parts, so in the same way the body of the universe is composed in its entirety of these parts."*

Diodorus' statements highlight:

- The Egyptian concept that the neteru (gods/goddesses) are the forces of nature and not actual characters
- The importance of the four elements of creation.
- The human body is a miniature universe.

Osiris represents the embodiment (emanation) of the moon, reflecting the light of the Isis The Sunshine.

11.1f. Isis: The Fertile Mother Earth—The Four Elements of Creation

The four elements of creation represent the four elements necessary to matter. Egyptians used the four simple phenomena (fire, air, earth and water) to describe the functional roles of the four elements necessary to matter. Isis represents the fertile aspect of Mother Earth.

The four elements of the world (water, fire, earth, and air), as quoted from Diodrus:

> **"As the Egyptians regard the Nile as the effusion of Osiris, so they hold and believe the earth to be the body of Isis, not all of it, but so much of it as the Nile covers, fertilizing it and uniting with it. From this union they make Horus to be born. The all conserving and fostering Hora, that is the seasonable tempering of the surrounding air, is Horus.**
>
> **The insidious scheming and usurpation of Seth [Typhon], then, is the power of drought, which gains control and dissipates the moisture which is the source of the Nile and of its rising."**

11.1g. Isis' Star—Sirius

As far back as the very remote periods of the Ancient Egyptian history, Isis has been associated with the star Sirius, the brightest star in heaven, which is called, like her, *the Great Provider* and whose annual rising ushers in the Nile's inundation and the beginning of the Egyptian

Sothic Year. It occurs when Sirius rises on the horizon together with the sun, and remains visible for a few moments until it fades with the advance of dawn.

Egypt's ingenious and very accurate calendar was based on the observation and the study of Sirius's movements in the sky. This fact is clearly acknowledged in the Webster's dictionary, which defines the Sothic year as:

– of having to do with Sirius, the Dog Star
– Designating or of an Ancient Egyptian cycle or period of time based on a fixed year.

[Read more about this subject in *Egyptian Cosmology: The Animated Universe*, by Moustafa Gadalla.]

11.1h. Isis' Twin Sister

In the Ancient Egyptian texts, the king declares that he owes his sovereignty to the favor of the sisters pair Isis and Nephthys. Duality for the Egyptians does not center on polarity, conflicts or divisiveness. The Egyptian concept of duality emphasizes the principle of the one-ness of the two, or the two that compliment or complete each other to become one.

The twin sisters are mirror images of each other. Isis represents the part of the world that is visible, while Nephthys represents that which is invisible.

Isis and Nephthys respectively represent the things that are and the things that are yet to come into being—the beginning and the end; birth and death.

On the cosmic level, Isis represents multiplication, fertility, and the enlarging womb of a mother or the huge enlarging bubble that we call the universe. Her sister Nephthys ensures the orderly and harmonic expansion by establishing outer boundaries or limitations on the expansion. They both ensure an orderly enlargement and contraction of the divine forces between the Big Bang and the Big Crunch.

On the universal level, Isis represents the active expanding womb that is called the universe, and her twin sister Nephthys represents the outer limits or perimeter of the universal bubble.

Isis symbolizes birth, growth, development and vigor.

Nephthys represents death, decay and immobility. Nephthys is associated with the coming into existence of the life that springs from death.

Isis and Nephthys are always associated inseparably with each other, and in all the important matters that concern the welfare of the deceased. They act together, and they appear together in Egyptian bas-reliefs and vignettes.

Since As Above So Below... the dual action of the two sisters on the cosmic level ... is found on Earth, one of their dual manifestations is their representation of fertility in the land of Egypt. Isis represents the fertile portions of Earth, while her sister, Nephthys, represents the barren perimeter of fertility. In his *Moralia Vol. V*, Plutarch explains:

> "...the Egyptians hold and believe the earth to be the body of Isis, not all of it, but so much of it as the Nile covers, fertilizing it and uniting with it. . . . The outmost parts of the land beside the mountains and bordering on the sea the Egyptians call Nephthys . This is why they give to nebt-het the name of "Finality"".

Isis, in several of her 10,000 names, is called:

> *Creator of green things.*
> *Lady of abundance.*
> *Lady of Green Crops.*
> *The Green Netert, Uatchet.*

At the end of the green areas that are full of life is Nephthys, whose name of finality means *complete, conclusive,
settled*, etc.

Isis and her sister, Nephthys, represent the limitation of
the fertile earth. Life, as represented by Isis, took place in
the active green areas while the Egyptians were buried on
the out-skirting areas of the barren land—the domain of
the sister Nephthys. Both sisters represent the common
saying *"from earth to earth"*.

[See more about Nephthys, later this chapter].

Isis: The Virgin Mother of 'God'

The very thing that is now called the Christian religion
was already in existence in Ancient Egypt long before the
adoption of the New Testament. The British Egyptologist, Sir E. A. Wallis Budge, wrote in his book, *The Gods of
the Egyptians* [1969]:

> *"The new religion (Christianity) which was preached
> there by St. Mark and his immediate followers, in all
> essentials so closely resembled that which was the out-
> come of the worship of Osiris, Isis, and Horus."*

The similarities, noted by Budge and everyone who has
compared the Egyptian Osiris/Isis/Horus allegory to the
Gospel story, are striking. Both accounts are practically
the same; e.g. the supernatural conception, the divine
birth, the struggles against the enemy in the wilderness,
and the resurrection from the dead to eternal life. The
main difference between the "two versions" is that the

Gospel tale is considered historical and the Osiris/Isis/Horus cycle is an allegory.

The spiritual message of the Ancient Egyptian Osiris/Isis/Horus allegory and the Christian revelation is exactly the same.

[For more information about allegories and especially the Universal Egyptian allegory of Isis-Osiris-Horus Allegory and its multi-dimensional meanings, read any/all of the references listed at the end of this book.]

Other aspects of this allegory can be found in this book, as follows:

> – Divine and Immaculate Conception—see Horus in previous chapter
> – The Divine Sacrifice—see Apis in previous chapter

More comprehensive information are to be found by books authored by Moustafa Gadalla, such as: *Ancient Egyptian Roots of Christianity* and/or *Isis: The Divine Female*.

Isis' Multitude of Attributes

The divine female principle of Isis manifests itself into numerous feminine-related attributes, and therefore the ancient Egyptians called her Isis of the 10,000 Names (meaning attributes). This was affirmed by Plutarch, where he writes in his *Moralia Vol. V*:

> *". . ., since, because of the force of Reason. Isis turns herself to this thing or that and is receptive of all manner of shapes and forms".*

Since Isis represents the universal female principle, she is manifested into numerous forms. It is therefore that she is described in the Ancient Egyptian texts as:

Isis of the 10,000 names [meaning] attributes
She of many names.

Here we present several various manifestations of the female principle in her various attributes, in alphabetical orders of such female "deities."

––––––

11.2 ANAT

As one of the manifestation of Isis, Anat represents the motherhood aspect of guardianship. The symbol of a mother protecting her offspring is the most powerful representation. A good guard is always ready to deter any outside threat. Therefore, Anat is represented as a woman holding a shield and an axe.

Anat is associated with Sekhmet—the lion-headed netert (goddess); the Fearless One.

––––––

11.3 BAST (BASTET—OUBASTIS)

Bast is one of several various manifestations of the female principle in her various attributes.

In the *Litany of Re*, Re is described as **The one of the cat** and **The great cat**. The nine realms of the universe are manifested in the cat; for both the cat and the grand Ennead (meaning the nine-times-unity) have the same ancient Egyptian term—Bast.

This relationship has found its way into western culture, where one says that *the cat has nine lives*.

Bast represents the gentle and docile aspect of the cat as opposed to Sekh-mut, the fiery lioness.

Bast is usually depicted as cat-headed.

Bast represents the total harmony within—the sense of internal happiness, contentment, and peace.

Herodotus wrote about the annual festivities around the Bast temple of Tell Basta (Bubastis), just outside Zagazig, in the Nile Delta. The annual festivities of this ancient city attracted more than 700,000 people. Herodotus described their joy during the Bast celebrations.

————

11.4 HATHOR (HET-HOR, HET-HERU, VENUS, APHRODITE, ASTRATE/ASERA/SERAH/SARAH)

Hathor is one of several various manifestations of the female principle in her various attributes.

Hathor is commonly translated by western Egyptologists as *"house of Horus"*. The first part, *Het/Hat*—translated as *"house"*- has a larger meaning than a *simple house*. It actually means the *womb* as a *Matrix*, within which something originates, takes form, and develops into full maturity.

The womb provides nourishment and protection. As such, Hathor provides both nourishment and protection—as we will see throughout the text.

Horus represents the realized divine principle—and Horus is recognized by various names/attributes as he develops from infancy to maturity within the cosmic womb.

Hathor represents the matrix of the metaphysical/spiritual principle, providing spiritual nourishment, healing, joy, lovemaking, music, and cheerfulness.

The Ancient Egyptian texts describe Isis of the 10,000 names in her role of Hathor as:

The Cow Heru-sekha, who brings forth all things.
Who nourished the child Horus with her milk.
Lady of joy and gladness.
Lady... of Love...

We will cover, here, the following subjects about her:

1. Lady Love—Venus
2. The Cosmic Nourisher—Madonna — cows symbolism
3. The Heavenly Seven Maidens
4. Hathor The Healer
5. Her Tree of Life
6. The Ultimate Shrine—'House of Horus/Re-horakhti'
7. Travelers Escort—Asrtarte
8. Notre Dame—Our Holy Mother of the Sea

1. Lady Love—Venus

The dictionary tells us that the origin of the name [or

word] Venus is *WENOS*. Wenos or *Wanas* is actually an Egyptian word meaning animated companionship–genial, sociable, cheerful and pleasurable. The noun form of we-nos is *A-nesa*, meaning maiden ... with all that it implies.

The Egyptian Venus, in her all-encompassing name of Hathor, represents the matrix of the metaphysical/spiritual principle providing spiritual nourishment, healing, joy, lovemaking, music and cheerfulness.

2. The Cosmic Nourisher

As the Great provider of spiritual nourishment, Hathor is often depicted as a cow-headed woman, or entirely in human form but with cow ears.

The cow is the ideal representation for nourishment of all kinds and, as such, is the ideal symbol for Het-Heru (Hathor).

On the cosmic level, Hathor is depicted in full cow form to symbolize the cosmic concept/attribute of nourishment.

We will highlight here a few cow forms of Hathor. First, Hathor as the Celestial cow Mehet-Uret, with her body spangled with stars.

Mehet-Uret (Mehurt, Methyer) represents the primeval water; i.e. the watery abyss of heaven.

Mehet-Uret is associated with Isis in her form of Hathor, representing both the physical and metaphysical nourishment.

Water is the source of life and sustenance.

Sometimes the king as symbol for Horus is shown taking milk from her udder.

The Ancient Egyptian texts describe Isis of the 10,000 names in her role of Hathor as:

> *The Cow Heru-sekha, who brings forth all things.*
> *Who nourished the child Horus with her milk.*

The Celestial cow is also depicted in seven cows. Hathor is associated with the number seven and was referred to as *The Seven Hathors.*

——

Hesat is a form of Hathor, whose function it is to feed the youngsters.

Hesat represents the metaphysical nourishment (love, caring, singing, etc.) necessary for the growth and well-being of the children.

The breast-feeding depiction represents both the physical as well as the metaphysical—spiritual nourishment. The most profound depiction is that of Isis in her form of Hathor, breast-feeding Baby Horus.

The Ancient Egyptian texts describe Isis of the 10,000 names in her role of Hathor as:

"Who nourished the child Horus with her milk".

This powerful representation served as the icon for The Madonna and the Child. The Egyptian Madonna and her child are found in Egyptian works since at least the Old Kingdom era 5,000 years ago, as shown earlier in this chapter.

In many depictions, we find The Egyptian Madonna and her child are shown in seven copies—again, to represent *the Seven Hathor.*

Depictions in Egyptian temples of breast-feeding of young and older adults by Hathor represent spiritual nourishment—for we all need spiritual nourishment during our progression towards maturity.

Hathor, as the symbol of spiritual nourishment, also plays an important role in the transformational (funerary) texts, furnishing the spiritual nourishment required by the soul of the deceased.

3. The Heavenly Seven Maidens

Hathor is known as the mistress of dance and the mistress of music.

Hathor is associated with the seven natural tones of the diatonic scale and is/was called "***The Seven Hathors***".

[More about music and dance in The Enduring Ancient Egyptian Musical System by Moustafa Gadalla.]

Since Hathor represents the metaphysical aspects of the universe, she encompasses the seven heavenly realms.

Hathor is found depicted wearing a sistrum—a musical rattle—on her head.

The text of the hymn of the "*Song of the Seven Hathors*", in the Temple of Dendera, consists of seven stanzas; each of four lines.

The intimate relationship between music and the cosmos is clearly stated in one of the Seven Stanzas as follows:

> *The sky and its stars make music to you.*
> *The sun and the moon praise you.*
> *The neteru* (gods, goddesses) *exalt you.*
> *The neteru* (gods, goddesses)*sing to you*

The musical aspect of Hathor is symbolized by Merit.

Merit is the cosmic conductor/maestro who manages the notes and the flow of musical performances. The hand of Merit is the universal symbol of action. Musically, the fingers control the sound emitted from musical instruments. How you place fingers determines the tones. Therefore, fingers are the most logical way to express, write, and instruct music.

As a consequence, a certain note took its name from the string plucked or deadened by this finger. As such, fingers have often been used to describe the technique of striking, among the expressions of instrumental playing.

In Egypt (Ancient and Baladi), this conventional "finger movement" mode has been all that is needed to identify the different modes.

4. Hathor The Healer

Isis in the form of Hathor represents the cure-all; and, as such, mankind is always seeking her aid.

She protects and cares for and nourishes all creations … She uses her power graciously and successfully for all those who seek aid.

The populace of Egypt looked upon Isis as a patroness whose solicitude extended over the entire range of human needs.

Diodorus of Sicily, in *Book One*, describes the female caring qualities of Isis in her form as Hathor:

> *"The Egyptians say that she was the discoverer of many health-giving drugs. . . and was greatly versed in the SCIENCE OF HEALING. Consequently, now that she has attained immortality, she finds her greatest delight in the healing of mankind. . . and gives aid in their sleep to those who CALL upon her. . . plainly manifesting both her very presence and her beneficence towards men who ask for her help. In proof of this, they say that practically the entire inhabited world is their witness. . . in that it eagerly contributes to the honors of Isis because she manifests herself in healings. For standing above the sick in their sleep. . . she gives them aid*

for their diseases. . . and works remarkable cures upon such as submit themselves to her. . . and many who have been despaired of by their physicians because of the difficult nature of their malady are restored to health by her. . . while numbers who have altogether lost the use of their eyes or of some other part of their body, whenever they turn to her for help, are restored to their previous condition"

By far, the largest number of shrines throughout Egyptian history was and continues to be dedicated to Hathor. There is practically no locality (small or large) in Egypt that does not have a shrine for the *Saba Banat*, meaning Seven Hathors. Such shrines are visited weekly by most Baladi women of Egypt.

Hathor is present in practically all temples and tombs, such as Luxor (Thebes), Heliopolis, Memphis, Dendera, Abu Simbel, the mining regions of Sinai, and countless places between these major centers. Hathor's most prominent center was/is at Dendera.

Hathor temples were often healing centers. Hathor represents healing (a function also associated with Sekhmet). One of Dendera's most important roles was as a healing center where all manner of therapies were practiced – just like a hospital in our modern sense, more or less; but with more emphasis on healing the body and soul using all means, and not limited to surgical procedures.

The Ancient Egyptian tradition of the *Seven Hathors* lives on, with shrines throughout present-day Egypt. There is practically no locality (small or large) in Egypt that does not have a shrine for the *Saba Banat*, meaning Seven

Hathors. Such shrines are visited weekly by most Baladi women of Egypt.

5. Her Tree of Life

Hathor represents the metaphysical connections between our earthly existence and past ancestors. As such, Hathor represents the family tree.

People throughout the world refer to their "family tree". In Egypt, this term is fully understood as the residence of the departed ancestors. As such, people often write notes and attach them to the branches of the tree. The tree becomes the medium between the departed and the living.

Hathor, therefore, represents the (family) tree netert (goddess).

About the significance of Hathor's tree, Plutarch, in *Moralia Vol. V* (378, 68 G), states:

> *"Of the plants in Egypt they say that the persea is especially consecrated to the netert* (goddess)*Hathor*

because its fruit resembles a heart and its leaf a tongue."

Plutarch's statement is affirmed by numerous Ancient Egyptian depictions of Hathor springing from the Tree of Life to provide spiritual nourishment.

The universal rule of cause and effect—symbolized by the functions of the heart and tongue—is found on the Egyptian *Shabaka Stele* (716-701 BCE), as follows:

> *"The Heart and the Tongue have power over all . . . the neteru* (gods, goddesses)*, all men, all cattle, all creeping things, and all that lives. The Heart thinks all that it wishes, and the Tongue delivers all that it wishes."*

6. The Ultimate Shrine—House of Horus/Re-horakhti

Let us go over what Hathor represents, one more time. Hat-hor is commonly translated by western Egyptologists as "house of Horus". The first part, Hat/Het (translated as "house") has a bigger meaning than a simple house. It actually means the womb as a Matrix within which something originates, takes form, and develops into full maturity.

Horus represents the realized divine principle—and Horus is recognized by various names/attributes as he develops from infancy to maturity within the cosmic womb. The final destination is unification with the creator as Re. At this point, the realized soul becomes ReHor-akhti. It is therefore that Het-hor is called the *Lady of the West, residence of Horus*—as Re-Hor-achti.

7. Travelers Escort Asrtarte

Hathor has a prominent presence beyond the land of Egypt. Let us pause here again to see how and why her role is significant beyond the land of Egypt.

We have shown that the name and function of Hathor represents the cosmic womb. As such, Hathor provides both nourishment and protection, as we have showed throughout this presentation.

Beyond the earthly existence, Hathor plays an important role in the transformational texts, furnishing the spiritual nourishment and guidance required by the soul of the deceased as it travels across the cosmic sea.

Hathor/Astarte—like other Egyptian deities – is also commonly known as *Asera/Serah/Sarah*, which means *noble lady*.

To leave no doubt of her Egyptian origin, Aserah is always portrayed in her Egyptian form with a crescent and disk on her headdress.

On Earth, Hathor provides a divine escort to travelers across the seas. Consequently, Hathor (also known as *Aserah*) is the Egyptian patroness of travel and sailing; and as a result, she appears in this role more often outside of Egypt.

An Egyptian coffin text (number 61) which is dated about 4,000 years ago describes her as *Hathor ... the lady who is said to 'hold the steering oars of barks'.*

Hathor's head is therefore always depicted right above the stern of ships where the twin rudders are mounted, which expert pilots use to guide the vessel. Guiding in the right direction is depicted here as the 4 oars with the *seven cows*—symbol of the *Seven Hathors*.

In her role as a guardian of travelers, Hathor is also called *Astarte*. Her temples are found at border cities, being that she is a patroness of travelers. The role of Astarte in Ancient Egypt is well documented and evident from documents from the time of Ramses II, which are about 3,300 years old. In one document, the role of Astarte as the seafarer's patroness is clearly stated:

> *.... BEHOLD... Astarte dwells in the region of the sea . . .*

To leave no doubt of her Egyptian origin, Astarte is always portrayed in her Egyptian form with a crescent-and-disk on her headdress, as shown above.

In another fragment, the Egyptian netert/goddess Renenutet addresses Astarte:

> *Behold, if thou bringest him tribute, he will be gracious unto thee. . .Therefore give him his tribute in silver, gold, lapis lazuli, and. . . wood.*

And she said unto the Ennead of neteru (gods/goddesses):

> *. . . the tribute of the sea; may he hearken unto us. . . .*

8. Notre Dame—Our Holy Mother of the Sea

A most prominent festival in southern France is held at the seaside by the Mediterranean Sea, towards the end of spring. This pilgrimage is the oldest in France and its destination is the church of Notre Dame de la Mer. The name of the church is ancient Egyptian.

notre (means our holy or goddess), dame [Da-meh] (dame means the mother), and de la mer (means water body or sea).

Thus, **notre dame de la mer** means **our holy mother of the sea**.

The "historical" tradition associated with this festival has a solid connection to Egypt. According to tradition, a dark-skinned Egyptian maiden called Saint Sarah arrived in a tiny boat without oars or sail, together with two white-skinned maidens whose names are Mary Salome and Mary Jacobe. Their boat is said to have landed on this part of the Mediterranean coast about Year 42 of our common era, having drifted across the Mediterranean sea from Egypt. This is one of numerous places throughout the countries of the Mediterranean Basin where festival traditions are Egyptian in origin—despite the apparent Christian origins of such festivals.

————-

11.5 HEKET (HEQET)

Heket is one of several various manifestations of the female principle in her various attributes.

Heket represents conception and procreation; i.e. she is the source of life. Therefore, she is generally found next to 'divine conception' scenes in Egyptian monuments.

Heket is depicted as a frog-headed woman or as a frog.

Frog amulets were/are popular for fertility because of the frog's prolific nature.

———————

11.6 KADESH (QADESH)

Kadesh is one of several various manifestations of the female principle in her various attributes.

Kadesh represents legitimacy.

Kadesh means holy or sacred, in Ancient Egyptian.

Kadesh is often represented as a young woman standing on a lion's back, signifying the matrilineal/matriarchal principle.

Kadesh is ordained and described in Ancient Egyptian texts as the **Beloved of Ptah**.

Kadesh is also associated with Hathor in her role as Astrarte, Patroness of travelers. It is therefore that we find the very same depiction here from Memphis more than 4000 years ago. We find similar depictions in Yemen at the southern end of the Red Sea in later times. This shows the vigorous sea trading during Ancient Egypt times, thousands of years ago.

———

11.7 MAAT (MAYET)

Maat is one of several various manifestations of the female principle in her various attributes. Ma-at represents the principle of cosmic order—the concept by which not only men, but also the neteru (gods, goddesses) themselves are governed. Ma-at signifies harmony, balance, and equilibrium between all the cosmic forces of nature (neteru).

Ma-at is usually portrayed as a woman wearing a headdress with an ostrich plume attached.

The concept of Ma-at has permeated all Egyptian writings from the earliest times and throughout Egyptian history. It is the concept by which not only humankind but also all the powers in the universe are governed. Maat signifies harmony, balance, and equilibrium between all the cosmic forces of the universe.

Ma-at is not easily translated or defined by one word. Basically, we might say that it means that which, of right, should be; that which is according to the proper order and harmony of the cosmos and of neteru (gods, goddesses) and men who are part of it. Ma-at could be favorably compared with the Eastern concept of karma and the Western concept of common sense.

Ma-at represents the abstract concept of order, justice, truth, righteousness, and what is right, in all their purest forms. Ma-at is the ideal of balance; of things working as they should. Without Maat, chaos reigns unchecked, and the ability to create order is forever lost. That is to say: Ma-at is order in its most abstract level—that which causes everything to exist and to continue to exist.

In human terms, Ma-at represents the right thing to do.

The application of the Ma-at principle extends to every aspect of Egyptian life. Being the model for cosmic harmony, order, balance, and equilibrium, Ma-at is associated with many functions.

We will briefly mention a few such applications:

1. Maat's Cosmic Role in

   – the pre creation planning
   – the dual nature of creation
   – the orderly plan of creation

2. Maat and the Earthly Voyage

   – Daily Activities and Temple Rituals
   – The Harmonic Laws of Music
   – Societal Order
   – The Spiritual Path
   – Justice for All—On Earth and After Earth

1. Maat as the World Order

Ma-at is the netert (goddess) that represents the principle of cosmic order.

We will briefly mention Maat's role in:

   a. the pre creation planning
   b. the dual nature of creation
   c. the orderly plan of creation

1a. Maat in the Pre-Creation Planning

For the deeply religious people of Egypt, the creation of the universe was not a physical event (Big Bang) that just happened. The explosion (Big Bang) that led to the creation of the universe was an orderly event, unlike all other explosions that exhibit a random and disordered form. Maat symbolizes the orderly Divine Law that governs the physical and metaphysical aspects of the world.

So, we read in the *Book of Knowing the Creations of Re and Overcoming Apep (Apophis)*, known as the *Bremner-Rhind Papyrus*:

> *"I had not yet found a place upon which I could stand. I conceived the Divine Plan of Law or Order (Maa) to make all forms. I was alone, I had not yet emitted Shu, nor had I yet emitted Tefnut, nor existed any other who could act together with me"*

The Egyptian texts emphasize again and again that the concept and details of creation was pre-planned according to an orderly form before the actual creation occurred.

1b. The Dual Nature of Creation — Maati

The Egyptians perceived the universe in terms of a dualism between Ma-at—Truth and Order—and disorder. The creation of the cosmos was summoned out of undifferentiated chaos, distinguishing the two by giving voice to the ultimate ideal of Truth. Ma-at, as shown here, is usually portrayed in the double form—Maati.

1c. The Orderly Plan of Creation

The Ancient Egyptian papyrus known as the *Bremn-erRhind Papyrus* tells us that before the creation took place, the master of the universe conceived the Divine Plan of Law or Order to make all forms:

> *"I conceived in my own heart; there came into being a vast number of forms of divine beings as the forms of children and the forms of their children".*

In the most simple terms, the Egyptian text tells us that the created world is basically a hierarchy of energies. This hierarchy is interrelated, and each level is sustained by the level below it. This hierarchy of energies is set neatly into a vast matrix of deeply interfaced natural laws, represented in the form of children and their children.

Ma-at represents the principle of cosmic order—the concept by which not only men but also the neteru (gods, goddesses) themselves are governed. Ma-at signifies harmony, balance and equilibrium between all the cosmic forces of nature (neteru).

2. Maat and the Earthly Voyage

  a. Daily Activities and Temple Rituals
  b. The Harmonic Laws of Music
  c. Societal Order
  d. The Spiritual Path
  e. Justice for All—On Earth and After Earth

2a. Daily Activities and Temple Rituals

As the model for cosmic harmony, order, balance, and equilibrium, Ma-at is associated with many functions such as all the activities of the Egyptian life, including building temples devoted to the maintenance of Ma-at.

The temple's rituals were based upon and coordinated with the movements of the heavens which were, in turn, manifestations of the divine cosmic law.

2b. Ma-at governs the harmonic laws of music.

Being the model for cosmic harmony, order, balance, and equilibrium, Ma-at is associated with many functions, such as the harmonic laws of music.

Music is all about balance. To maintain Ma-at is to maintain harmony, balance, and equilibrium in everything—including music. Ma-at's representations are found as "decoration" on many Egyptian instruments. The experts in music were called musicians/priests of Ma-at, and teaching instruments were/are called Mizan—meaning balance/scale.

Ma-at is usually depicted next to the typical Ancient Egyptian scale with two unequal weights, therefore requiring balancing by the plumb bob. The plumb bob determines the vertical and governs the equilibrium of the scales. Scenes of weighing show that it is necessary to still the plumb line, because otherwise it would continue to oscillate. The Ancient Egyptian term for oscillation, intoxication, and plumb bob is tkh.

The plumb bob, tkh, is very often modeled in the form of the heart, ib, the Dancer. The heartbeat provides us with a convenient measure of time.

2c. Maat as the Societal Order

Ma-at is related to societal orderly harmonic relationships.

In order to achieve perfect universal harmony, the social structure must mirror the same orderly hierarchy of the created universe. [Read about this subject matter in Egyptian Cosmology:The Animated Universe, by Moustafa Gadalla]

2d. Maat as the Spiritual Path

As the model for cosmic harmony, order, balance, and equilibrium, Ma-at represents the spiritual path that each individual must follow.

Ma-at is maintained in the world by the correct actions and personal piety of its adherents. The ultimate objective of earthly man is to develop his/her consciousness to the utmost perfection. This means that he/she becomes harmoniously tuned with nature.

Ma-at represents the spiritual path that each individual

must follow. The Egyptian model recognizes the uniqueness of each individual, and as such recognizes that the paths to the divine are as numerous as the number of seekers. The ways to the divine are like streams—they all go to one source. As it is shown throughout this presentation, the Ancient Egyptians implemented their beliefs in individuality in all their texts. As shown earlier, there were never two identical transformational (funerary) or medical (so-called "magical") texts for any two individuals. One must live his or her own life, and each one of us must go his or her own way, guided by ma-at.

[More information in *Egyptian Cosmology: The Animated Universe* and *Egyptian Mystics: Seekers of the Way,* both by Moustafa Gadalla.]

2e. Maat as Lady Justice—Both on Earth and After Earth

Being the model for cosmic harmony, order, balance, and equilibrium, Ma-at is associated with many functions, such as the administration of justice both on Earth and after Earth.

Ma-at is the Egyptian *lady of justice.* Our symbol of modern-day justice is a blindfolded lady carrying a scale. Such symbolism is derived from ma-at, the ancient Egyptian's symbol of justice—a blindfolded lady. Ma-at is depicted in her role as lady of justice as "*having her eyes closed*" to ensure equal justice for all.

Ma-at is often shown in a double form representing the two opposing sides of litigation because the scale of justice cannot balance without the equality of opposing forces.

Judgment Day is held in what the Egyptians called the Hall of Two Maati.

The Egyptian lady of justice is portrayed as a woman with her symbol, the ostrich feather, mounted on her head, holding the emblem of truth to emphasize the main concept of justice—search for The truth.

The Ma-at symbol is the feather of truth/ostrich feather used in the scale of justice.

As attested to by Diodorus: All judges of high rank in Ancient Egypt were described as priests of Ma-at, and the chief justice wore a little figure of Ma-at around his neck as a badge of office.

Judgment Day—Hall of the Two Maati

The ultimate objective of the earthly man is to develop his/her consciousness to the utmost perfection. This means that he/she becomes harmoniously tuned with nature. This was symbolized in some Egyptian tombs by the deceased soul reciting the 42 Negative Confessions, on the Judgment Day, before the 42 jurors/neteru. The successful person was declared, by the Grand Jury as Maa Kheru—True of Voice, to be Sound.

The soul of the deceased is led to the Hall of Judgment of the Double-Ma-at. She is double because the scale balances only when there is an equality of opposing forces. Ma-at's symbol is the ostrich feather, representing judgment or truth. Her feather is customarily mounted on the scales.

Anubis, as opener of the way, guides the deceased to the

scales and weighs the heart. The heart, as a metaphor for conscience, is weighed against the feather of truth to determine the fate of the deceased.

Maintain Maat.

––––––

11.8 MERIT

Merit is one of several various manifestations of the female principle in her various attributes, as manifested in Hathor [shown above].

Merit represents the orderly harmonic sequence, or process. Merit establishes cosmic order by means of her gestures. As such, she is/was referred to as a chironomist netert (goddess) who manages the notes and the flow of musical performances. She is the Cosmic Maestro.

.Ancient Egyptian tombs and temples yield several series of choreographic, rhythmic, and melodic hand signs that correspond to certain signs of chironomids. The tones are presented by different positions of the arms and fingers (forefinger against the thumb, the stretched out hand, etc.), resulting in an absolute correspondence between tonal steps of the Ancient Egyptian musical system and hand signs.

Merit represents the musical hand—with all that implies.

[For information about music in Ancient Egypt, read *The Enduring Ancient Egyptian Musical System* by Moustafa Gadalla.]

————

11.9 MUT

Mut is one of several various manifestations of the female principle in her various attributes.

The term Mut is connected linguistically with the many similar-sounding words for *mother*, found in many languages.

Mut is usually depicted as a woman, with the body of the vulture so artfully formed to her own head that it passes for a headdress. Sometimes Mut is shown with feathered, winged, outstretched arms.

The reasons for choosing the vulture for this particular feminine role are:

– The vulture is supposed to be particularly zealous in caring for its young.
– The female vulture gets impregnated by exposing herself to male sperm carried by the winds, and not through direct contact with males. The vulture is therefore a symbol of virgin birth—in other words, purity.

Mut is found in many places and in many forms.

Mut is associated with Sekhmet, Hathor, Nut, and with Bast, among many others.

———————

11.10 NEPHTHYS (NEBT-HET)

Nephthys is one of several various manifestations of the female principle in her various attributes.

Her Name and Headdress

Nephthys is portrayed as a woman wearing upon her head the symbols that are read as her name. Nephthys, in her purely Egyptian form, is actually two words – Nebt-Het – which means:

– golden/noblest/mistress (Nebt), of the place/house (Het).

Nephthys is one of the four canopic jar patrons, protecting the lungs.

Isis protects the liver.

Serket protects the intestines.

Net (Neith) protects the stomach.

Nephthys: Isis' Twin Sister

In the Ancient Egyptian texts, the king declares that he owes his sovereignty to the favor of the sisters Isis and Nephthys. Duality for the Egyptians does not center on polarity, conflict,s or divisiveness. The Egyptian concept of duality emphasizes the principle of the one-ness of the two, or the two that compliment or complete each other to become one.

The twin sisters are mirror images of each other. Isis represents the part of the world that is visible, while Nephthys represents that which is invisible.

Isis and Nephthys respectively represent the things that

are and the things that are yet to come into being—the beginning and the end; birth and death.

On the cosmic level, Isis represents multiplication, fertility, and the enlarging womb of a mother—or the huge, enlarging bubble that we call the universe. Her sister Nephthys ensures orderly and harmonic expansion by establishing outer boundaries or limitations on expansion. They both ensure an orderly enlargement and contraction of the divine forces between the Big Bang and the Big Crunch.

On the universal level, Isis represents the active expanding womb that is called the universe, and her twin sister Nephthys represents the outer limits or perimeter of the universal bubble.

Isis symbolizes birth, growth, development and vigor. Nebt-het represents death, decay and immobility. Nephthys is associated with the coming into existence of the life that springs from death. Isis and Nephthys are always associated inseparably with each other and in all the important matters that concern the welfare of the deceased. They act together and they appear together in Egyptian bas-reliefs and vignettes.

Since As Above So Below, the dual action of the two sisters on the cosmic level is found on Earth, and one of their dual manifestations is their representation of fertility in the land of Egypt. Isis represents the fertile portions of earth, while her sister, Nephthys, represents the barren perimeter of fertility. In his *Moralia Vol. V*, Plutarch explains:

> *". . .the Egyptians hold and believe the earth to be the body of Isis, not all of it, but so much of it as the Nile covers, fertilizing it and uniting with it. . . . The outmost parts of the land beside the mountains and bordering on the sea the Egyptians call nebt-het. This is why they give to Nephthys the name of "Finality"*

Isis, in several of her 10,000 names, is called:

> *Creator of green things.*
> *Lady of abundance.*
> *Lady of Green Crops.*
> *The Green Netert, Uatchet*

At the end of the green areas that are full of life is Nephthys, whose name of finality means complete—conclusive—settled.

Isis and her sister, Nephthys, represent the limitation of the fertile Earth. Life, as represented by Isis, took place in the active green areas while the Egyptians were buried on the out-skirting areas of the barren land, the domain of the sister Nephthys. Both sisters represent the common saying *"from earth To earth"*:

> *The Two Ladies and The Diadem*

The twin sisters had a major role in king making. In one of the many attributes of Isis, she is called,

The Maker of Kings.

Isis, who delivers the king his rank, without whom no king can exist.

In the Ancient Egyptian texts, the King declares that he owes his sovereignty to the favor of the Sisters Pair, Isis and Nephthys. Their symbolic representations are found on the famous diadems worn by the Egyptian Pharaohs.

One Egyptian title of the Kings was Lord of the diadem of the vulture and of the serpent. The diadem, combining the serpent and vulture, was the earthly symbol of the divine man, the King. The diadem consisted of the serpent, the symbol of divisive intellectual functions; while the vulture was the symbol of the reconciliation functions. The divine man must be able to distinguish and to reconcile. Since these dual powers reside in humankind's brain, the form of the serpent's body follows the actual physiological sutures of the brain in which these particularly human faculties are seated.

Located in the middle of the forehead, the diadem represents the third eye, with all its metaphysical powers.

The diadem consisted of:

The serpent or cobra—known primarily as Uatchet—representing the potent fertile creative power of Isis. And the vulture—known as Nekhebet—representing the barrenness, namely, Nephthys.

The mighty cobra which can swallow a huge animal and digest it was, for the Egyptians, the earthly manifestation of the divine intellect. The faculty of intellect allows a person to break down a whole complex issue or body into its constituent parts in order to digest it.

The intellectual symbolism of the cobra is complimented by the vulture's primordial reconciliation. Reconciliation is also a female aspect of the universe.

This is the female dual nature, as represented by the Twin Sisters.

———————

11.11 NEITH [NET]

Neith is one of several various manifestations of the female principle in her various attributes.

A few of the 10,000 attributes of Isis call her:

Lady of the shuttle.

Isis, Weaver and Fuller.

In the allegory of Isis and Osiris, Isis collected the scattered pieces of her beloved Osiris and assembled and knitted them together. Her knitting and weaving show the underlying metaphysical qualities of establishing patterns. In such a role, she is recognized as Net, or Neith, representing the divine process of setting harmonic patterns as symbolized by the act of weaving.

The Egyptian pronunciation of the name—being *Net*—tells a lot; for to knit or nit/net in English means to establish a pattern fabric from two directions. Net is portrayed as a woman carrying two crossed arrows. She wears a weaving shuttle upon her head. Weaving is accomplished by the crossing of nerves and fibers. These two arrows represent the two directions of crossing.

Net/Neith represents the ability to establish a pattern—the creating of a netted fabric by weaving or determining the pattern of behavior of someone or something.

Not coincidentally, Net/Neith is one of the four canopic jar patrons and protector of the stomach, which is the seat of process, and digestionboth physically and metaphysically.

———————

11.12 NUT

Nut is one of several various manifestations of the female principle in her various attributes.

The Firmament of Heaven

As a consequence of the Big Bang, the firmament was formed. The firmament as heaven is described in ancient Egypt as the sky, viewed poetically as a solid arch or vault. The ancient Egyptian texts describe Isis as:

> **Queen of heaven.**

> **Queen of the Firmament.**

In her role as the firmament, Isis is recognized as Nut. Nut is depicted in several forms; but often as a naked woman arched over the heavens, in the act of swallowing the evening sun and giving birth to the morning sun. The new sun is often shown in its form of the scarab beetle.

Nut represents the sky as matrix of all—the cosmic source of nourishment.

Nut and Geb—The Celestial Sphere

Duality is the natural manifestation of creation. In this light, Nut as a female principle has a mirror image counter male partner. Nut's male counterpart is Geb. Geb represents the material/physical aspects of the universe.

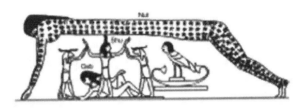

Geb is depicted as a man bearing a goose upon his head. This representation is the source of the worldwide notion about the goose that laid the golden egg—from which the world was hatched. In scientific terms, the egg is the celestial sphere—the universal bubble that contains all creation. In this celestial sphere, Geb represents the phenomenal or physical world and Nut represents the noumenal or metaphysical world.

Nut The Heavenly Astronomical Starry Sky

Nut is depicted as a star studded woman arched over the heavens.

Strikingly, in the first book of Genesis, we read:

> *"And God said, Let there be lights in the firmament of the heaven".*

Genesis I, 14 reads:

> *"14: And God said, Let there be lights in the firmament of the heaven to divide the day from the night; and let*

them be for signs, and for seasons, and for days, and years:

The implications here are that the changes observed in the sky are correlated to changes on Earth, such as the seasonal cycles.

The cyclical nature of the universe—in whole or in part—is a constant and consistent theme in the Ancient Egyptian texts. Nut is depicted arched over the heavens in the act of swallowing the evening sun and giving birth to the morning sun. The new sun is often shown in the form of scarab beetle—a new beginning; a rebirth.

Reference to the creation of the stars is given at the end of Genesis I, 16 &in I, 17:

16: And God made two great lights; the greater light to rule the day, and the lesser light to rule the night: he made the stars also.

17: And God set them in the firmament of the heaven to give light upon the earth.

For the Ancient Egyptians, the stars have much more significance than to just "give light upon the earth."

The Egyptian Nut is always associated with the constellations in the sky. Most noticeable are the zodiac signs that are found in Egyptian tombs and temples many centuries before the Greek era.

Nut the Spirit of the Sky

Nut as the Spirit of the Sky is prominently depicted in the

resting places of the Ancient Egyptians— in the coffin lids as well as in tomb chambers.

And for these successful souls—after their earthly existence—Nut springs out from the tree of life to offer them the everlasting metaphysical nourishment.

––––––

11.13 SATIS (SATET)

Satis is associated with Sirius, the star of Isis that ushered in the beginning of the Ancient Egyptian New Sothic Year and the Nile inundation season. [See Isis, above, in this chapter.]

Satis is associated with Khnum [see Khnum, in the previous chapter, for more details about the role of time-keeping].

Satis is depicted as a woman wearing the white crown with antelope horns.

––––––

11.14 SEKHMET (SEKH-MUT, SAKHMET, PETESACHMIS)

Sekhmet is one of several various manifestations of the female principle in her various attributes.

Sekhmet or Sekhmut is actually two words: Sekh and Mut—meaning *Elder* or the *Den Mother*.

As the Den Mother, Sekh-Mut is portrayed as a lioness in Egyptian representations. Sekhmet statues are usually made of igneous rocks, such as basalt or granite, emphasizing her PASSIONATE fiery nature.

Sekhmet represents the fiery aspect of the creative power.

In the *Litany of Re*, Ra (Re) is described (in one of his 75 forms/attributes) as *The One of the Cat*, and as *The Great Cat*.

As the Divine Den Mother, Sekh-Mut is usually portrayed as a woman with exposed breasts and the head of a lioness, surmounted by the sun's disk, around which is a uraeus.

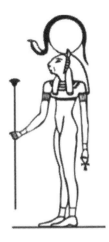

As the Divine Den mother, she projects:

- an urge/passion/desire/will to create
- passionate tender loving care
- passionate fearless protection of her creation

To present her urge/passion/desire/will to create, Sekh-Mut is depicted with an ithyphallic male body.

Sekh-Mut is almost always depicted with Khonsu; she representing the female solar principle and he—Khonsu-representing the male lunar principle.

Sekh-Mut is depicted in many places showing her passionate tender loving care; support and encouragement.

To show her passionate fearless protection of her creation, Sekh-Mut statues are found at the entry point to temples—such as in Medinet Hapu in Luxor or depicted on the outer wall of the temple in Esna.

The lioness is the most fearless animal on earth. In our modern societies, the guts and spine are symbols of physical courage. This concept has Ancient Egyptian roots. In the *Papyrus of Ani* [pl.32 item 42], we read:

"*my belly and my spine are Sekh-Mut*"

— — — — —

11.15 SELKIS (SERKET, SELKIT, SERQET)

Selkis is one of several manifestations of the female principle in her various attributes.

Selkis represents the zealous protection aspect of motherhood.

Selkis is identified with the scorpion, which is famous for its protection of its young.

Selkis, as an aspect of Isis, represents the protection and nurturing of young children.

Selkis is usually depicted as a woman with a scorpion on her head, or sometimes as a scorpion with a woman's head.

Selkis is one of the patrons of the four canopic jars, protecting the intestines.

11.16 SESHAT (SAFKHET, SESAT, SESHET, SESHETA, SESHATA)

Seshat is one of several manifestations of the female principle in her various attributes.

Seshat represents the organizational capacity of keeping records—knowledge, information, etc.

Seshat is depicted carrying the reed pen and palette, and records deeds in eternity/space; i.e. memory.

Seshat (or Sefekht, meaning seven) is usually depicted wearing the panther skin—denoting primordial power—and a seven-petaled flower on her head.

Seshat is referred to as: *The Enumerator, Lady of Writing(s), Scribe, Head of the House of the Divine Books (Archives),* and *Lady of Builders.*

She is commonly shown in scenes depicting the laying of the foundation of a new temple. In this regard, she is described as the Lady of Builders.

Seshat is closely associated with Thoth, and is considered to be a female counterpart of Thoth.

As the keeper of records, Seshat is usually depicted at scenes of Tree of Life recordings.

———————

11.17 TAURT (TAWERET, THOERIS, TOERIS)

Isis (in the form of Ta-urt) is described in Ancient Egyptian texts as the "mistress of the gods" and "bearer of the gods". Ta-urt is thus the patroness of children and maternity. She represents the Midwife par excellence—both physically and metaphysically.

Ta-urt is found at the beginning of each cycle, such as the zodiac cycle, as depicted in numerous places prior to the Greek era.

Ta-urt is portrayed as an upright hippopotamus with pendulous breasts, lion's paws, and a crocodile's tail.

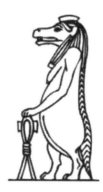

Ta-urt or Thoueri is also known under the "names" Apet/Opet and Sheput. In her form of Ipet/Opet/Apet, Ta-urt plays a crucial role in the largest temple in Egypt (namely, the Karnak Temple complex at Luxor [Thebes]).

The Ancient Egyptian name for the Karnak temple itself is **Apet-sut**, which means **Enumerator of the Places**.

The design and enumeration in this temple are consistent with the creation and growth numerical codes. The principles and applications of such numerical and geometrical codes are detailed in another segment that deals with Egyptian Temples: Heaven on Earth.

One of the most prominent festivals in Luxor, since ancient times, is the Apet Festival.

Scenes from an Apet Feast celebrated during the reign of Tutankhamen, decorate the walls of a colonnade in the Luxor temple, and give a lively impression of the occasion.

The Ancient Egyptian name for Luxor is **T-Apet,** and one needs say no more.

———

11.18 TEFNUT

Tefnut is actually two words—*Tef* and *Nut*.

Tef means spit or spittle. Such an expression is even common among present English-speaking people. When we say "a spitting image", we mean "exactly like." The very same meaning is applicable in case of *Tef – nut*—meaning this/she who spat Nut.

Nut being the firmament, which is detailed in another segment of this Program.

Spittle is moisture and Tef-nut represents the moisture—one of the two primary agents that were needed for the creation of the universe. The other agent is the heat, represented in the Ancient Egyptian texts as Shu, Tef-nut's counterpart. It is very difficult to talk about either one in isolation, and therefore we will be talking about the dual Tef-nut and Shu.

Tefnut   Shu

The pair of Tefnut and Shu is portrayed as a wife and husband.

The pair of husband and wife is the characteristic Egyptian way of expressing duality and polarity. This dual nature was manifested in Ancient Egyptian texts and traditions from its recovered archaeological findings.

The initial dual principle in the creation state was expressed in the pair of Shu and Tefnut.

The most ancient texts of the Old Kingdom, namely the

Pyramid Texts §1652, express this dual nature:

"...and though didst spit out as Shu, and didst spit out as Tefnut."

This is a very powerful analogy, because we use the term "spitting image" to mean "exactly like the origin".

Creation was the result of the Big Bang. The created universe is subject to two opposing

1) the expulsion forces, which cause all galaxies to move away from us.

Shu represents this force. Shu, represented by fire, air, and heat, corresponds to the quality of expansiveness, rising, centrifugal forces, positive, masculine, outgoing, outward extroversion, etc.

2) the opposing force to expulsion and expansion is a contractional force, which pulls the galaxies together.

Tefnut symbolizes this contraction force—a female aspect of the universe to bring things together; the Den Mother.

Tefnut, represented by moisture, and the objective material basis of manifestation (Nut, the suffix) corresponds to contraction, downward movement, centripetal forces, negative, feminine, receptive, inner, introspection, etc.

Heat (Shu) and water (Tefnut) are the two most universal shaping factors of lifeforms. These terms correspond to fire (heat) and moisture, respectively, and are to be understood as metaphors and actual correspondences for the abstract qualities that they represent.

The outer limits of the expanding bubble are the firmament—the sky that is viewed poetically as a solid arch or vault, depicted in Ancient Egypt as Nut.

In the Ancient Egyptian texts, Shu and Tefnut are described as the ancestors of all the neteru (gods/goddesses) who begat all beings in the universe.

CHAPTER 12 : THE ARCHETYPAL SYNERGIES

12.1 ASSOCIATIONS AND MANIFESTATIONS

The energies represented by the various neteru (gods/goddesses) rarely function individually, but are often allied or fused with other neteru (gods/goddesses). The union of certain pairs of complementary energies/attributes (masculine and feminine forms) results in a third energy/attribute. Trinities are sometimes portrayed together as a single composite entity; sometimes separately and sometimes in binary form.

In human terms, a family consists of a man, a woman, and a child. The three are one unit—a family. There are also binary relationships such as: husband–wife (marriage), father–child (fatherhood), and mother–child (motherhood).

Egyptian deities are connected in a complex and shifting array of relationships. A neter's connections and interactions with other deities helps define its character. Such relationships were the base material from which Egyptian allegories were formed.

A distinction must be made between associations of deities and manifestations of a neter principle into other neteru's principles/forms. For example, it is wrong to assume that Re-Sebek is an association of two deities. When we realize what Re REPRESENTS, then we can figure out that Re-Sebek is the manifestation of the creation force [being Re] into the Sebek form/aspect. As mentioned earlier, the *Litany of Re* shows his manifestation into 75 forms/aspects.

Synergetic combinations were not permanent. A neter/ netert who was involved in one combination continued to appear separately and formed new combinations with other deities.

The combined synergies are basically found in dual, triple, octad and ennead combinations, to be detailed as follows:

12.2 DUALITIES

The universal dual nature of creation manifests itself in various applications, as identified in Ancient Egypt. Each dualizing aspect of the creation process is represented by two divine attributes—neteru. Depending on each specific aspect, the dualizing neteru [but always a solar and lunar combination] may be:

- A female and a male
- 2 females
- 2 males
- 2 halves of unisex

Some dualities were discussed throughout this book. For detailed information, read *Egyptian Cosmology: The Ani-*

mated Universe [Third Edition] by Moustafa Gadalla, where you will find a detailed discussion of several dualities; the three distinctive areas being:

A. Creation—Formative Aspects
- Pre-creation Twin gendered Dualities
- Shu and Tefnut—The Bubble Makers
- Isis and Nephthys—Twin Sisters
- Maati
- Re & Thoth
- Isis & Osiris—The Dynamic Dual
- Seth—including w/Maat w/Horus w/Osiris w/Ptah

B. Unification Aspects
- The "Two Plants"
- Horus & Thoth
- Two Hapis [Unisex]
- Qareens of the Two Lands

C. Cyclical Aspects
- Osiris & Horus
- Re & Osiris
- Aker—Twin Lions

12.3 TRINITIES

The Ancient Egyptians recognized the significance of trinity in the creation process. As such, Ancient Egyptian texts rendered the trinity as a unity expressed by the singular pronoun—it is the Three that are Two that are One.

The principles of creation are unity, duality and trinity. This is made clear in the Ancient Egyptian papyrus known as the *Bremner-Rhind Papyrus*:

"After having become one neter (god)*, there were [now]
three neteru* (gods, goddesses) *in me ..."*—referring to
the triad of Atum and the dual Shu-and Tefnut.

The various trinities are related to various nature of the
duality within each trinity.

Some trinities were discussed throughout this book. For
more detailed examples, read *Egyptian Cosmology: The
Animated Universe* [Third Edition] by Moustafa Gadalla.

12.4 OGDOADS

At number 8, we find the human being created in the
image of God, the First Principle. Our earthly existence
at the 8th realm is a replication and not a duplication—an
octave. An octave is the future state of the past. The continuance of creation is a series of replications—octaves.
Eight, then, corresponds to the manifested physical world
as we experience it.

In Egypt, the well-known text *Coffin of Petamon* [Cairo
Museum item no. 1160] states:

> *I am One who becomes Two,
> who becomes Four,
> who becomes Eight,
> and then I am One again.*

This new unity (One again) is not identical, but analogous, to the first unity (I am One). The old unity is no
longer, a new unity has taken its place: The King is Dead,
Long Live the King. It is a renewal or self-replication. And
to account for the principle of self-replication, 8 terms are
necessary.

Eight is the number of Thoth and at Khmunu (Hermopolis). Thoth (aka Hermes/Mercury) is called the ***Master of the City of Eight***.

Thoth was the messenger of the neteru (gods, goddesses) of writing, language, and of knowledge. Thoth gave man access to the mysteries of the manifested world, which were symbolized by the number Eight.

Stanza 80 of the Ancient Egyptian *Leiden Papyrus J350* retraces the Creation as told in Khmunu (Hermopolis), which deals with the Ogdoad—the Primordial Eight which comprised the first metamorphosis of Amon-Re, the mysterious, hidden one who is recognized as Ta-Tenen at Men-Nefer (Memphis); then Ka-Mut-f at Ta-Apet (Thebes) – yet all the while remaining One.

Therefore, the manifestation of creation in 8 terms is present in all four Ancient Egyptian cosmological centers:

- At Memphis, Ptah, in his 8 forms, created the universe.

- At Heliopolis, Atam created the 8 divine beings.

- At Khmunu (Hermopolis), 8 primeval neteru—the Ogdoad—created the universe. They were the representation of the primeval state of the universe.

- At Luxor (Thebes), Amun/Amen after creating himself in secret, created the Ogdoad.

The manifestation of creation through 8 terms is also reflected in the mystical process of squaring the circle. [See the details in an earlier chapter as it relates to the duality of Re &Thoth].

Pre-creation Twin gendered Dualities

Egyptian texts state that Nun—the pre-creation chaos—possessed characteristics that were identified with four pairs of primordial powers/forces. Each pair represents the primeval dual-gendered twins—the masculine/feminine aspects.

The four males of the pairs are represented as frogs. The four females of the pairs are represented as serpents. The eight beings are depicted with their legs tied, indicative of their essential nature as being action; but while in the subjective realm (before creation), they are inert. Having their legs tied represents their potential energies.

12.5 ENNEDS

Number nine marks the end of gestation and the end of each series of numbers. If multiplied by any other number, it always reproduces itself (3 x 9 = 27 and 2 + 7 = 9 or 6 x 9 = 54 and 5 + 4 = 9 and so on).

Nine marks the transition from one scale (the numbers from 1 to 9) to a higher scale (starting with 10), and so it is the number of initiation, which is again similar to the birth of a baby after nine months.

A human child is normally conceived, formed, and born in nine months; a fact which has a good deal to do with the role and importance attached to the number nine in ancient Egypt.

Correspondingly, the Ancient Egyptian refers to a group of nine divinities as one unit—being an Ennead. As stated earlier, we find that as far back as at least 5000 years ago, the Pyramid Texts reveal the existence of three companies of gods, and each company consisted of 9 neteru (gods, goddesses).

The Egyptian texts speak of three Enneads—each representing a phase in the creation cycle.

The nine aspects of an Ennead are not a sequence, but a unity—interpenetrating, interacting, and interlocked.

[For more information about number mysticism in Egypt, read *Egyptian Cosmology: The Animated Universe* by Moustafa Gadalla.]

GLOSSARY

---

ankh – the symbol of eternal life.

Animism – the concept that all things in the universe are animated (energized) by life forces. This concurs, scientifically, with the kinetic theory, where each minute particle of any matter is in constant motion; i.e. energized with life forces.

ba – usually translated as the soul. It is the divine, immortal essence. When the ba departs, the body dies. The ba is usually shown as a stork with a human head.

Baladi – the present silent majority of Egyptians that adhere to the Ancient Egyptian traditions, with a thin exterior layer of Islam. The Christian population of Egypt is an ethnic minority that came as refugees from Judaea and Syria to the Ptolemaic/Roman-ruled Alexandria. 2,000 years later, they are easily distinguishable in looks and mannerisms from the majority of native Egyptians.

BCE – Before Common Era. Also noted in other references as BC.

Book of Coming Forth By Light (Per-em-hru) – consists of over one hundred chapters of varying lengths, which are closely related to the Unas Transformational/Funerary (so-called Pyramid) Texts at Sakkara. This book is to be found, in its complete form, only on papyrus scrolls that were wrapped in the mummy swathings of the deceased and buried with him/her.

Book of the Dead – see Book of Coming Forth By Light.

canopic jar – special jars or receptacles used to store the vital organs of the deceased.

carrion – dead and putrefying flesh.

CE – Common Era. Also noted in other references as AD.

cosmology – the study of the origin, creation, structure, and orderly operation of the universe as a whole; and of its related parts.

Djed – see Tet.

Duat/Tuat – the Underworld, where the soul of the deceased goes through transformation leading to resurrection.

ithyphallic – with phallus erect. [Read more about it under Min.]

matriarchy – A society/state/organization whose descent, inheritance, and governance are traced through the females. It is the woman who transmits political rights, and the husband she chooses then acts as her executive agent.

matrilineal – A society whose descent, inheritance, and governance are based on the maternal line.

neter/netert – a divine principle/function/attribute of the One Great God. Incorrectly translated as god/goddess.

papyrus – could mean either: 1) A plant that is used to make a writing surface. 2) Paper, as a writing medium. 3) The text written on it, such as the Bremner-Rhind Papyrus.

Persea – a sacred tree, probably a form of avocado.

Pyramid Texts – a collection of transformational (funerary) literature that was found in the tombs of the 5th and 6th Dynasties (2465-2150 BCE).

scarab – amulet in the form of a black beetle, a symbol of formation. Also see 'Khepri' throughout the text.

scepter – an ornamented rod or staff; a symbol of sovereignty.

stele (plural: stelae) – stone or wooden slab or column bearing textual inscriptions.

Tet – a symbolic column or pillar representing the backbone of Osiris, the support of creation.

uraeus – rearing cobra.

was (ouas) – a scepter, often with animal head, signifying dominion.

SELECTED BIBLIOGRAPHY

Baines, John, and Jaromir Málek. *Atlas of Ancient Egypt*. New York, 1994.

Budge, E.A. Wallis. *Egyptian Religion: Egyptian Ideas of the Future Life*. London, 1975.

Budge, E.A. Wallis. *The Gods of the Egyptians*, 2 volumes. New York, 1969.

Budge, Wallis. *Osiris & The Egyptian Resurrection* (2 volumes). New York, 1973.

Egyptian Book of the Dead (The Book of Going Forth by Day), The Papyrus of Ani. USA, 1991.

Gadalla, Moustafa:
– *Ancient Egyptian Culture Revealed*. USA, 2007.
– *Egyptian Cosmology: The Animated Universe—2nd edition*. USA, 2001.
– *Egyptian Divinities: The All Who Are THE ONE*. USA, 2001.
– *Egyptian Harmony: The Visual Music*. USA, 2000.
– *Egyptian Mystics: Seekers of the Way*. USA, 2003.
– *The Ancient Egyptian Roots of Christianity*. USA, 2007.
– *Egyptian Rhythm: The Heavenly Melodies*. USA, 2002.
– *Egyptian Romany: The Essence of Hispania*. USA, 2004.

– *Historical Deception: The Untold Story of Ancient Egypt*. USA, 1999.

Herodotus. *The Histories*, tr. A. de Selincourt. New York and Harmondsworth, 1954.

James, T.G.H. *An Introduction to Ancient Egypt*. London, 1979.

Kastor, Joseph. *Wings of the Falcon, Life and Thought of Ancient Egypt*. USA, 1968.

Piankoff, Alexandre. *The Litany of Re*. New York, 1964.

Piankoff, Alexandre. *The Pyramid of Unas Texts*. Princeton, NJ, USA, 1968.

Piankoff, Alexandre. *The Shrines of Tut-Ankh-Amon Texts*. New York, 1955.

Plato. *The Collected Dialogues of Plato including the Letters*. Edited by E. Hamilton & H. Cairns. New York, 1961.

Plotinus. *The Enneads, in 6 volumes*, Tr. By A.H. Armstrong. London, 1978.

Plotinus. *The Enneads*, Tr. By Stephen MacKenna. London, 1991.

Plutarch. *Plutarch's Moralia, Volume V*. Tr. by Frank Cole Babbitt. London, 1927.

Siculus, Diodorus. *Vol 1*. Tr. by C.H. Oldfather. London.

Wilkinson, Sir J. Gardner. *The Ancient Egyptians, Their Life and Customs*. London, 1988.

Numerous references written in Arabic.

Several Internet sources.

TRF PUBLICATIONS

Tehuti Research Foundation (T.R.F.) is a non-profit, international organization, dedicated to Ancient Egyptian studies. Our books are engaging, factual, well researched, practical, interesting, and appealing to the general public. Visit our website at:

https://www.egypt-tehuti.org
E-mail address: info@egypt-tehuti.org

The publications listed below are authored by T.R.F. chairman,
Moustafa Gadalla.

The publications are divided into three categories:

[I] Current Publications in English Language
[II] Earlier Available Editions in English Language
[III] Current Translated Publications in Non English Languages[Chinese, Dutch, Egyptian(so-called "arabic"), French,German, Hindi, Italian, Japanese, Portuguese, Russian & Spanish]

[I] Current Publications in English Language

The Untainted Egyptian Origin—Why Ancient Egypt Matters

ISBN-13(pdf): 978-1-931446-50-1
ISBN-13(e-book): 9781931446-66-2

This book is intended to provide a short concise overview of some aspects of the Ancient Egyptian civilization that can serve us well nowadays in our daily life no matter where we are in this world. The book covers matters such as self empowerment, improvements to present political, social, economical and environmental issues, recognition and implementations of harmonic principles in our works and actions, etc.

———

The Ancient Egyptian Culture Revealed, *Expanded 2ⁿᵈ ed.*

ISBN-13(pdf): 978-1-931446-66-2
ISBN-13(e-book): 978-1-931446-65-5
ISBN-13(pbk.): 978-1-931446-67-9

This new expanded edition reveals several aspects of the Ancient Egyptian culture, such as the very remote antiquities of Egypt; the Egyptian characteristics and religious beliefs and practices; their social/political system; their cosmic temples; the richness of their language; musical heritage and comprehensive sciences; their advanced medicine; their vibrant economy; excellent agricultural and manufactured products; their transportation system; and much more.

———

Isis : The Divine Female

ISBN-13(pdf): 978-1-931446-25-9
ISBN-13(e-book): 978-1-931446- 26-6
ISBN-13(pbk.): 978-1-931446-31-0

This book explains the divine female principle as the source of creation (both metaphysically and physically); the feminine dual nature of Isis with Nephthys; the relationship (and one-ness) of the female and male principles; the numerology of Isis and Osiris; Isis' role as the Virgin Mother; explanation of about twenty female deities as the manifestations of the feminine attributes; the role of Isis' ideology throughout the world; the allegory of Isis, Osiris and Horus; and much more. This book will fill both the mind with comprehensive information as well as the heart with the whole spectrum of emotions.

—

Egyptian Cosmology, The Animated Universe*, Expanded 3rd edition*

ISBN-13(pdf): 978-1-931446-44-0
ISBN-13(e-book): 978-1-931446-46-4
ISBN-13(pbk.): 978-1-931446-48-8

This new expanded edition surveys the applicability of Egyptian cosmological concepts to our modern understanding of the nature of the universe, creation, science, and philosophy. Egyptian cosmology is humanistic, coherent, comprehensive, consistent, logical, analytical, and rational. Discover the Egyptian concept of the universal energy matrix and the creation process accounts. Read about numerology, dualities,trinities, numerical significance of individual numbers thru the number ten; how the human being is related to the universe; the Egyptian astronomical consciousness; the earthly voyage; how the social and political structures were a reflection of the universe; the cosmic role of the pharaoh; and the interactions between earthly living and other realms; climbing the heavenly ladder to reunite with the Source; and more.

Egyptian Alphabetical Letters of Creation Cycle

ISBN-13(pdf): 978-1-931446-89-1
ISBN-13(e-book): 978-1-931446-88-4
ISBN-13(pbk.): 978-1-931446-87-7

This book focuses on the relationship between the sequence of the creation cycle and the Egyptian ABGD alphabets; the principles and principals of Creation; the cosmic manifestation of the Egyptian alphabet; the three primary phases of the creation cycle and their numerical values; and the creation theme of each of the three primary phases, as well as an individual analysis of each of the 28 ABGD alphabetical letters that covers each letter's role in the Creation Cycle, its sequence significance, its sound and writing form significance, its numerical significance, its names & meanings thereof, as well as its peculiar properties and its nature/impact/influence.

Egyptian Mystics: Seekers of the Way, Expanded 2nd ed.

ISBN-13(pdf): 978-1-931446-53-2
ISBN-13(e-book): 978-1-931446-54-9
ISBN-13(pbk.): 978-1-931446-55-6

This new expanded edition explains how Ancient Egypt is the origin of alchemy and present-day Sufism, and how the mystics of Egypt camouflage their practices with a thin layer of Islam. The book also explains the progression of the mystical Way towards enlightenment, with a coherent explanation of its fundamentals and practices. It includes details of basic training practices; samples of Ancient Present Egyptian festivals; the role of Isis as the 'Model Philosopher'.It shows the correspondence between the Ancient Egyptian calendar of events and the cosmic cycles of the universe; and other related miscellaneous items.

Egyptian Divinities: The All Who Are THE ONE, *Expanded 2ⁿᵈ ed.*

ISBN-13(pdf): 978-1-931446-57-0
ISBN-13(e-book): 978-1-931446-58-7
ISBN-13(pbk.): 978-1-931446-59-4

This new expanded edition shows how the Egyptian concept of God is based on recognizing the multiple attributes of the Divine. The book details more than 100 divinities (gods/goddesses); how they act and interact to maintain the universe; and how they operate in the human being—As Above so Below, and As Below so Above.It includes details of the manifestations of the neteru (gods, goddesses) in the creation process; narrations of their manifestations; man as the universal replica; the most common animals and birds neteru; and additional male and female deities.

The Ancient Egyptian Roots of Christianity, *2nd ed.*

ISBN-13(pdf): 978-1-931446-75-4
ISBN-13(e-book): 978-1-931446-76-1
ISBN-13(pbk.): 978-1-931446-77-8

This new expanded edition reveals the Ancient Egyptian roots of Christianity, both historically and spiritually. This book demonstrates that the accounts of the "historical Jesus" are based entirely on the life and death of the Egyptian Pharaoh, Twt/Tut-Ankh-Amen; and that the "Jesus of Faith" and the Christian tenets are all Egyptian in origin—such as the essence of the teachings/message, as well as the religious holidays.It also demonstrates that the major biblical ancestors of the biblical Jesus—being David, Solomon and Moses are all Ancient Egyptian pharaohs as well as a comparison between the creation of the universe and man (according to the Book of Genesis) and the Ancient Egyptian creation accounts.

The Egyptian Pyramids Revisited, *Expanded Third Edition*

ISBN-13(pdf): 978-1-931446-79-2
ISBN-13(e-book): 978-1-931446-80-8
ISBN-13(pbk.): 978-1-931446-81-5

The new expanded edition provides complete information about the pyramids of Ancient Egypt in the Giza Plateau. It contains the locations and dimensions of interiors and exteriors of these pyramids; the history and builders of the pyramids; theories of construction; theories on their purpose and function; the sacred geometry that was incorporated into the design of the pyramids;

and much, much more. It also includes details of the interiors and exteriors of the Saqqara's Zoser Stepped "Pyramid" as well as the three Snefru Pyramids that were built prior to the Giza Pyramids. It also discusses the "Pyramid Texts" and the works of the great pharaohs who followed the pharaohs of the Pyramid Age.

———————

The Ancient Egyptian Metaphysical Architecture, *Expanded Edition*

ISBN-13(pdf): 978-1-931446-63-1
ISBN-13(e-book): 978-1-931446-62-4
ISBN-13(pbk): 978-1-931446-61-7

This new expanded edition reveals the Ancient Egyptian knowledge of harmonic proportion, sacred geometry, and number mysticism as manifested in their texts, temples, tombs, art, hieroglyphs, etc., throughout their known history. It shows how the Egyptians designed their buildings to generate cosmic energy; and the mystical application of numbers in Egyptian works. The book explains in detail the harmonic proportion of about 20 Ancient Egyptian buildings throughout their recorded history.It also includes additional discussions and details of the symbolism on the walls; the interactions between humans and the divine forces; Egyptian tombs, shrines and housing; as well as several miscellaneous related items.

———————

Sacred Geometry and Numerology,

ISBN-13(e-book): 978-1-931446-23-5

This document is an introductory course for learning the fundamentals of sacred geometry and numerology, in its true and complete form, as practiced in the Egyptian traditions.

The Egyptian Hieroglyph Metaphysical Language

ISBN-13(pdf): 978-1-931446-95-2
ISBN-13(e-book): 978-1-931446-96-9
ISBN-13(pbk.): 978-1-931446-97-6

This book covers the Egyptian Hieroglyph metaphysical language of images/pictures; the language of the mind/intellect/divine; the scientific/metaphysical realities of pictorial images (Hieroglyphs) as the ultimate medium for the human consciousness that interpret, process and maintain the meanings of such images; how each hieroglyphic image has imitative and symbolic (figurative and allegorical) meanings; the concurrence of modern science of such multiple meanings of each image; how Egyptian hieroglyphic images represent metaphysical concepts; and the metaphysical significance of a variety of about 80 Egyptian Hieroglyphic images.

The Ancient Egyptian Universal Writing Modes

ISBN-13(pdf): 978-1-931446-91-4
ISBN-13(e-book): 978-1-931446-92-1
ISBN-13(pbk.): 978-1-931446-93-8

This book will show how the Egyptians had various modes of writings for various purposes, and how the Egyptian modes were falsely designated as "separate languages" belonging to others; the falsehood of having different languages on the Rosetta (and numerous other similar) Stone; and evaluation of the "hieratic' and "demotic" forms of writing. The book will also highlight how the Egyptian alphabetical language is the MOTHER and origin of all languages (as confirmed by all writers of antiquities) and how this one original language came to be called Greek, Hebrew, Arabic and other 'languages' throughout the world through the deterioration of sound values via 'sound shifts', as well as foreign degradation of the original Egyptian writing forms.

────────

The Enduring Ancient Egyptian Musical System—Theory and Practice, Expanded Second Edition

ISBN-13(pdf): 978-1-931446-69-3
ISBN-13(e-book): 978-1-931446-70-9
ISBN-13(pbk.): 978-1-931446-71-6

This new expanded edition explains the cosmic roots of Egyptian musical and vocal rhythmic forms. Learn the fundamentals (theory and practice) of music in the typical Egyptian way: simple, coherent, and comprehensive.It provides discussions and details of an inventory of Ancient Egyptian musical instruments explaining their ranges and playing techniques. It also discusses Egyptian rhythmic dancing and musical harmonic practices by the Ancient Egyptians and other miscellaneous items.

────────

Egyptian Musical Instruments, 2nd ed.

ISBN-13(pdf): 978-1-931446-47-1

ISBN-13(e-book): 978-1-931446-73-0
ISBN-13(pbk.): 978-1-931446-74-7

This book presents the major Ancient Egyptian musical instruments, their ranges, and playing techniques.

The Musical Aspects of the Ancient Egyptian Vocalic Language

ISBN-13(pdf): 978-1-931446-83-9
ISBN-13(e-book): 978-1-931446-84-6
ISBN-13(pbk.): 978-1-931446-85-3

This book will show that the fundamentals, structure, formations, grammar, and syntax are exactly the same in music and in the Egyptian alphabetical language. The book will show the musical/tonal/tonic Egyptian alphabetical letters as being derived from the three primary tonal sounds/vowels; the fundamentals of generative phonology; and the nature of the four sound variations of each letter and their exact equivalence in musical notes; the generative nature of both the musical triads and its equivalence in the Egyptian trilateral stem verbs; utilization of alphabetical letters and the vocalic notations for both texts and musical instruments performance; and much more.

Egyptian Romany: The Essence of Hispania, *Expanded 2nd ed.*

ISBN-13(pdf.): 978-1-931446-43-3
ISBN-13(e-book): 978-1-931446- 90-7
ISBN-13(pbk.): 978-1-931446-94-5

This new expanded edition reveals the Ancient Egyptian roots of the Romany (Gypsies) and how they brought about the civilization and orientalization of Hispania over the past 6,000 years. The book shows also the intimate relationship between Egypt and Hispania archaeologically, historically, culturally, ethnologically, linguistically, etc. as a result of the immigration of the Egyptian Romany (Gypsies) to Iberia.It alsp provides discussions and details of the mining history of Iberia; the effects of Assyrians and Persians attacks on Ancient Egypt and the corresponding migrations to Iberia; the overrated "Romans" influence in Iberia; and other miscellaneous items.

[II] Earlier Available Editions in English Language — continue to be available in PDF Format

Historical Deception: The Untold Story of Ancient Egypt, 2nd ed.

ISBN-13: 978-1-931446- 09-1

Reveals the ingrained prejudices against Ancient Egypt from major religious groups and Western academicians.

Tut-Ankh-Amen: The Living Image of the Lord

ISBN-13: 978-1-931446- 12-1

The identification of the "historical Jesus" as that of the Egyptian Pharaoh, Twt/Tut-Ankh-Amen.

Exiled Egyptians: The Heart of Africa

ISBN-13: 978-1-931446-10-5

A concise and comprehensive historical account of Egypt and sub-Sahara Africa for the last 3,000 years.

The Twilight of Egypt

ISBN-13: 978-1-931446-24-2

A concise and comprehensive historical account of Egypt and the Egyptians for the last 3,000 years.

[III] Current Translated Publications in Non English Languages [Chinese, Dutch, Egyptian (so-called "arabic"), French,German, Hindi, Italian, Japanese, Portuguese, Russian & Spanish]

Details of All Translated Publications are to be found on our website

---

14836550R00166

Printed in Germany
by Amazon Distribution
GmbH, Leipzig